Editor
Walter Kelly, M.A.

Managing Editor
Ina Massler Levin, M.A.

Editor-in-Chief
Sharon Coan, M.S. Ed.

Illustrator
John Pritchett

Cover Artist
Brenda DiAntonis

Art Manager
Kevin Barnes

Art Director
CJae Froshay

Imaging
Rosa C. See

Product Manager
Phil Garcia

Publishers
Rachelle Cracchiolo, M.S. Ed.
Mary Dupuy Smith, M.S. Ed.

Good Writing Grades 6-8

Ideas and Content • Word Choice • Fluency • Voice • Organization • Conventions • Presentation

Author

Tracie Heskett

Teacher Created Materials, Inc.
6421 Industry Way
Westminster, CA 92683
www.teachercreated.com

ISBN-0-7439-3359-1

©2004 Teacher Created Materials, Inc.

Made in U.S.A.

Table of Contents

Introduction

What Is Trait Writing?

In the early 1980s, teachers in the northwestern United States felt they needed a set of common guidelines by which to teach and assess student writing. By comparing student writing that needed extensive revision to student writing that did not, certain characteristics, or traits, emerged. The qualities found in successful student writing have been revised over time and are now commonly known as the traits of good writing. In keeping with current academic standards, teachers are including communication and presentation skills. The analytic traits identified for use in instructing and assessing student writing are contained in the list below:

- Ideas and Content (page 8)

- Word Choice (page 18)

- Fluency (page 27)

- Voice (page 36)

- Organization (page 46)

- Conventions (page 56)

- Presentation (page 68)

Why Should I Teach Trait Writing?

The trait-writing model allows teachers and students to focus on one element of writing at a time, thus breaking into manageable parts the task of learning to write effectively. The traits apply to a variety of writing styles and purposes. Most importantly, mastery of these traits gives students skills they can use for life.

How Do I Teach Trait Writing in the Classroom?

One trait can be presented each week for seven weeks; there are daily lessons for each trait. The teacher may also teach one entire trait on a single day as a comprehensive thematic unit. Lessons should be taught in sequence since many build on material already completed. Lessons in this book are directed to the students, who may read and work through the exercises on their own. Many of the exercises use graphic organizer pages to photocopy for the students. Have students use a notebook or save their writing in a folder or on a disk for future use. Students should skip a line in their writing exercises or double space; these drafts will be used in later lessons to provide editing practice.

Each trait includes a literature-based lesson, which introduces students to writing that exhibits one or more of the traits. Each lesson incorporates one or more academic standards. These standards are adapted with permission from *Content Knowledge: A Compendium of Standards and Benchmarks for K–12 Education*, ©2000, Mid-continent Research for Education and Learning.

Standards for Writing

Grades 6–8

> **1. Demonstrates competence in the general skills and strategies of the writing process**

A. Prewriting: Uses a variety of prewriting strategies (e.g., makes outlines, uses published pieces as writing models, constructs critical standards, brainstorms, builds background knowledge)

B. Drafting and Revising: Uses a variety of strategies to draft and revise written work

C. Editing and Publishing: Uses a variety of strategies to edit and publish a written work

D. Evaluates own and others' writing

E. Uses style and structure appropriate for specific audiences

F. Writes expository compositions

G. Writes narrative accounts (e.g., engages the reader by establishing a context and otherwise developing reader interests; establishes a situation, plot, persona, point of view, setting, and conflict; creates an organizational structure that balances and unifies all narrative aspects of the story; uses sensory details and concrete language to develop plot and character; excludes extraneous details and inconsistencies; develops complex characters; uses a range of strategies such as dialogue, tension or suspense, naming, and specific narrative action such as movement, gestures, and expressions)

H. Writes compositions about autobiographical incidents

I. Writes biographical sketches

J. Writes persuasive compositions

K. Writes compositions that speculate on problems/solutions

L. Writes in response to literature (e.g., anticipates and answers a reader's questions, responds to significant issues in a log or journal, answers discussion questions, writes a summary of a book, describes an initial impression of a text, connects knowledge from a text with personal knowledge)

M. Writes business letters and letters of request and response

Standards for Writing (cont.)

Grades 6-8

2. Demonstrates competence in the stylistic and rhetorical aspects of writing

  A. Uses descriptive language that clarifies and enhances ideas (e.g., establishes tone and mood, uses figurative language)

  B. Uses paragraph form in writing

  C. Uses a variety of sentence structures to express expanded ideas

  D. Uses some explicit transitional devices

3. Uses grammatical and mechanical conventions in written compositions

4. Gathers and uses information for research purposes

  A. Gathers data for research topics from interviews

  B. Organizes information and ideas from multiple sources in systematic ways (e.g., time lines, outlines, notes, graphic representations)

5. Demonstrates competence in speaking and listening as tools for learning

  A. Plays a variety of roles in group discussions (e.g., active listener, discussion leader, facilitator)

  B. Asks questions to seek elaboration and clarification of ideas

  C. Listens in order to understand a speaker's topic, purpose, and perspective

  D. Conveys a clear main point when speaking to others and stays on the topic being discussed

  E. Presents simple prepared reports to the class

  F. Listens to and understands the impact of nonprint media on media consumers (e.g., persuasive messages and advertising in media, the presence of media in people's daily lives, the role of the media in forming opinions, media as a source of entertainment and information)

  G. Identifies the ways in which language differs across a variety of social situations

Standards Table

Exercise	Standard	Page Number
Ideas and Content		8
Bicycling for Writers	1A, 4, 4B	10
Gathering Your Supplies	1A, 1B, 2A	12
Extreme Adventure	1B, 1D, 1H, 1L, 3, 4A	14
Obstacles on the Trail	1B, 1G, 2A, 3	15
Examine the Trail	1A, 1B, 1E, 1H	17
Word Choice		18
Shots That Make the Basket . . .	1A, 3	20
Counting Points	1B, 1D, 1E, 1L, 2A, 3	21
A Game Plan for Effective Writing	1A, 1E, 2A, 3	22
Photo Album	1A, 1B, 1G	23
Starring . . .	1A, 1C, 1E, 2A	24
Fluency		27
Splashing in Fluency	1A, 1B, 1G, 2, 3	29
What If . . . ?	1B, 1D, 1G, 5	30
Dance in the Water	1A, 2	31
Just Splashing Around	1A, 1B, 1D, 2A, 2C, 2D, 3	32
Different Strokes	1B, 1G, 2, 3	34
Voice		36
The Sounds of the Slopes	1B, 1G, 1K, 3	38
Whose Style?	1A, 1D, 1G	39
The Style and Voices of . . .	1B, 1D, 1G, 1L	42
Developing My Own Style	1A, 1B, 1E, 1H, 2	44
Snowboarding for Everyone	1B, 1C, 1E, 1M, 3	45
Organization		46
Finding Your Way Through the Game Plan	1A	48
What's the Strategy?	1A, 1D	49
The Kickoff . . . and the Goal	1A, 1D, 2D	50
Here's the Plan	1A, 1B, 1G, 1K, 2, 3	52
It's a Classic	1A, 1B, 1G, 2, 3, 5F	54
Conventions		56
Warming Up	1B, 1C, 1D, 1F, 3	59
The Pitch	1B, 1C, 1D, 3	60
You Swing . . .	1B, 1C, 1D, 1F, 2, 3	64
One Base at a Time	1B, 1C, 1D, 1G, 2, 3	65
Home Run	1B, 1C, 1D, 1G, 2, 3	66
Presentation		68
Introducing . . .	1H, 1I, 5F	70
Presenting . . .	1A, 1F, 2, 4, 4B, 5A, 5B, 5D, 5E	71
The Athletes Speak	1A, 1B, 1C, 1E, 1F, 5C, 5D, 5E, 5F	72
Track and Field—a Collage of Events	1C, 1E, 5C, 5D, 5E, 5F	74
Your Presentation	1C, 1D, 5A, 5B, 5C, 5F, 5G	75
All-Star Track Meet	1C, 1D, 2, 3, 5E, 5F	76

Ready, Set, Go!

On Your Way to Effective Writing
(introduction to the student)

The sports world has much to teach about the craft of writing. Sports give people the opportunity to be adventurous, to set goals and expectations, to participate in teamwork and competition, and to improve individual performance. In the same way, writing is an exercise, a sport. As you learn the sport of writing, you will create adventures, chart your progress as you meet goals, work with others and on your own, and improve your ability to communicate. Writing also contains an element of competition; every writer competes for his or her reader's attention. In these lessons, various sports are related to the characteristics found in effective writing.

Hands-on experience will enable you to develop your writing skills; these skills will help you as you complete other class assignments as well. The overall design of these lessons is to work through each of the exercises. Your teacher may assign some or all of the exercises; continue to practice and use those that work best for you. Since the lessons build on each other to some extent, keep the work that you do; some exercises are referred to in later sections. You will want to keep a writing journal or notebook and/or keep a folder on a floppy disk.

At the beginning of each exercise, there is an objective to keep in mind, a "Tip from the Coach." Also listed are any supplies, or "Equipment," you will need for that particular activity. Following this will be a section called "Trait Development." Each activity is designed to help you develop a particular trait of good writing—*ideas and content*, *word choice*, *fluency*, *voice*, *organization*, *conventions*, or *presentation*. Here in this section you will find the comments, explanation, and instructions for this activity. Finally, there are questions for you to reflect on, referred to as "Check Yourself," at the end of each exercise with space for you to make notes. These notes may be useful for you as you complete class assignments in writing and other subjects. Let the games begin as you pursue the goal of writing more effectively.

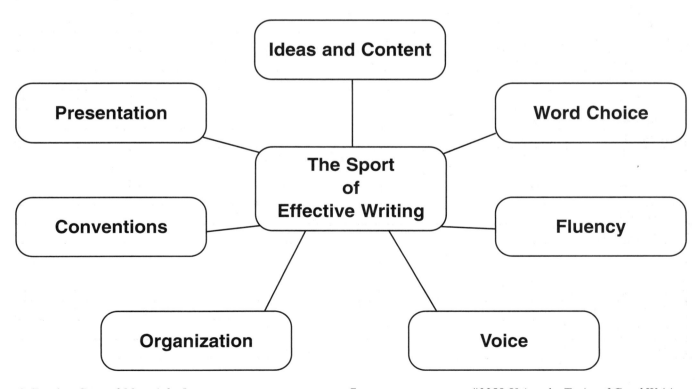

Ideas-and-Content Trait

The ideas-and-content trait helps students gather and organize ideas efficiently and use relevant details that add to the whole. Students learn to use what they know and present ideas clearly to the reader. The lessons that follow use mountain biking to illustrate the characteristics of this trait.

Before beginning a ride, a cyclist must gather any necessary gear and check the bike. Bicycles have many detailed, intricate parts. Each part serves a specific purpose relevant to the bike's operation. Bicycles range from simple, having basically a pedal and brake, to complicated, having numerous gears, shock absorbers, pegs, racks, etc. Learning to ride a bike may be painful and fearful, but once learned is never forgotten. The cyclist often surprises the spectator with what he knows, whether in freestyle or racing. These cycling characteristics all have strong parallels in writing.

Lessons begin with a research exercise in which students work with partners on a Venn diagram, using dictionaries and thesauri to compare biking with writing. This exercise familiarizes students with characteristics of the ideas-and-content trait. In the next two exercises, students generate a list of writing topics, select a topic from the list, and then use a graphic organizer to develop the idea further. They will incorporate relevant details, specific examples, related experiences, and their own knowledge of the topic. Encourage students to seek out new knowledge to add to what they already know.

In the third lesson, students examine a literature selection for qualities of the ideas-and-content trait, working in small discussion groups. They will then brainstorm ideas relating to their own experiences and write individual stories. The next exercise uses a graphic organizer to help develop insight and understanding. You may wish to introduce character development into the lesson to assist students who may feel uncomfortable using first person. Finally, students construct "story maps" of their lives, helping them gather previous experiences. Students will add to individual story maps in a later lesson.

Middle school students should be encouraged to explore topics, collecting ideas or information. Clear writing based on an author's experience, understanding, and insight invites any reader to continue. As in cycling, a well-written piece leads the reader to a satisfying, convincing conclusion. In good writing, nothing extraneous appears. Effective writing comes from adequate preparation, organization, and use of ideas—that is the essence of the ideas-and-content trait.

Ideas and Content

(to the student)

Ready, set, go! The race begins. As you set out on the trail, you see your friend riding up alongside you. He's going to get to the jump before you. This inspires you to press on to make the jump higher, to ride more effectively to win the race. These exercises will help you write more effectively, in a way that others will find interesting and enjoyable to read.

The first trait of good writing is called "ideas and content." This refers to gathering and organizing your ideas to use them efficiently. You will learn to use what you know and to present your ideas clearly to the reader. Don't hesitate to explore a topic. You will need to collect ideas and information about your topic. Use relevant details; make sure everything adds to the whole. Specific details and examples will help you prove your point. Write clearly, from your own experience. This will show insight and understanding, convincing your reader to keep turning pages for more.

Cyclists ride in many places and for a variety of reasons. Various types of bicycles have been developed for different purposes: cross country racing, downhill racing, touring, and freestyle, or trick riding, and others. Before beginning a ride, the cyclist must gather necessary gear and check the bike. Bicycles have many detailed, intricate parts. Each part serves a specific purpose in the bike's operation. Bicycles range from simple, having basically a pedal and brake, to complicated, with numerous gears, shock absorbers, pegs, racks, etc. As a cyclist, you need to be aware of your surroundings; as a writer, you need to be aware of your reader. Not watching the trail—or your writing—may result in an accident.

Learning to ride a bike may be painful and fearful, but once you learn, you never forget. Whether racing with friends or just doing tricks on your bike, you will often surprise those watching with what you know.

Develop Ideas and Content

- Generate an intriguing topic.
- Connect your writing to your own experience.
- Use interesting, relevant, specific details.
- Keep your reader in mind.
- Surprise the reader with what you know, using insight and understanding.
- Use clear ideas.
- Use examples; show, don't tell the reader what he already knows.
- Develop your story; every piece should add to the whole.

Bicycling for Writers

Equipment

- dictionary and/or thesaurus
- Mountain Biking for Writers, page 11

Trait Development

Think about riding a bike. Compare it to what you have read so far about the ideas-and-content trait. How will you prepare to write? Work with a partner, using a dictionary and/or thesaurus to help you compare biking to writing. Use key words and terms, such as pedal, tire, frame, wheels, pegs, etc. Use the diagram on page 11 of Mountain Biking for Writers to compare riding a bike to writing. When you have completed the diagram, turn back to this page and continue reading. Stop reading now.

Before you can successfully reach the end of the trail, you will need to know the trail, investigate the options, and become an expert. You will seek new knowledge by gathering information to add to what you already know. You will want to be prepared with specific details relevant to the task. You will find a topic or a trail on which to ride. Next, you will generate some ideas and gather your supplies. Then you will be ready to write with insight and understanding that will convince your reader to come along with you.

Check Yourself

Write three sentences comparing bicycling to writing. How will learning about the ideas-and-content trait help you in your writing? What aspect of this trait (refer to page 9 if necessary) will be the hardest for you to put into practice? What will be the easiest characteristic to incorporate into your writing?

My Notes

_____   _____

_____   _____

_____   _____

_____   _____

_____   _____

_____   _____

_____   _____

Mountain Biking for Writers

Directions: Use the diagram to compare writing to mountain biking. Think of important key words and terms about each topic, writing them in the appropriate portions of the diagram. Try to find some similarities as well, writing them in the overlapping portion of the diagram.

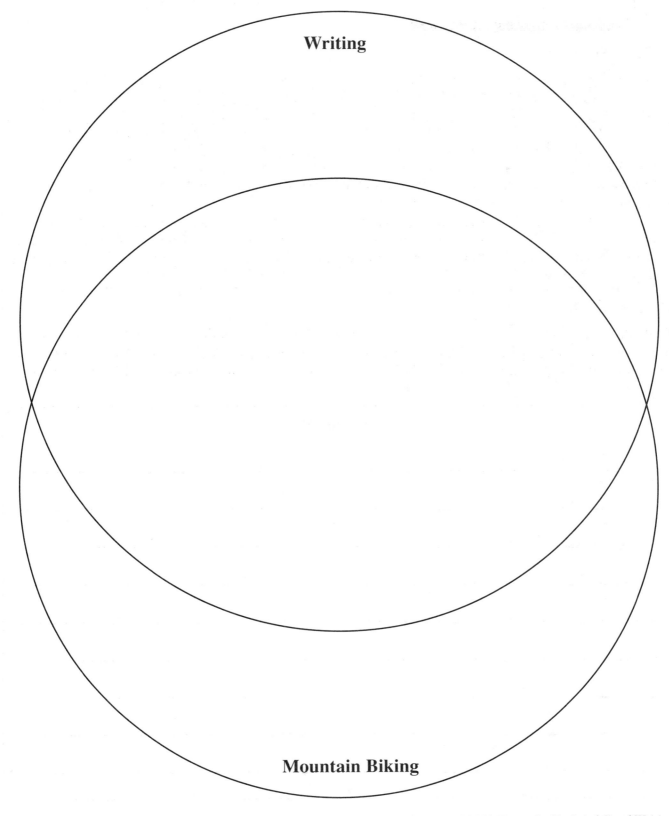

Gathering Your Supplies

Equipment

- Supply List #1, page 13
- Supply List #2, page 13

Trait Development

Look around. Are you ready? You probably have everything you need; make sure it is organized in such a way that you can use it. The content for a wonderful story is there—equipment to help you ride down the trail. You have your ideas, experiences, details, examples, insight, and understanding. Get your ideas down on paper. Begin with Supply List #1. Brainstorm and list as many story topics as you can. What do you know a lot about? Your writing will be more interesting if you write about what you know. You may need to explore and investigate to learn more about a particular subject in which you are interested. Collect information; write about your experiences. A reader wants to know more. Show your reader what you know.

Choose one topic or experience from your Supply List #1 on page 13. On Supply List #2, page 13, complete the graphic organizer for the topic you chose. Gathering your ideas and expanding on them will help you develop the content of your writing. Use this prewriting exercise as a plot for a story. As you write your story, remember to include relevant details and examples, as well as background knowledge to develop your story.

Check Yourself

Which topics on your list excite you enough to write about? Why do those particular ideas seem as if they might be successful or interesting story material?

My Notes

_____   _____

_____   _____

_____   _____

_____   _____

_____   _____

_____   _____

_____   _____

Supply Lists

List #1: Generating Topics

Directions: Use this half-page to brainstorm topics of interest to you. The pictures on the page may help you get started.

List #2: My Idea!

Directions: Use this half-page to organize and expand your ideas about one of your topics from List #1.

List #1:	Generating Topics

List #2:	My Idea

Extreme Adventure

Equipment

- literature sample, picture book: *BMX Bikes* by Barbara Knox. Capstone Press, 1996.
- chapter book option: *Olympic Dream* by Matt Christopher. Little, Brown, & Co., 1996.
- props, costumes, puppet-making supplies (*optional*)

Trait Development

(*Your teacher may have you work with a group for this exercise.*)

It helps to ride a familiar trail. Many authors draw on their past experiences in their writing. Read through the literature selection. Notice how the author incorporates experiences or makes connections from his or her life into the story.

Every element of writing should add something to the whole. Select sentences or passages from the book and discuss with your group how the story would change if those sentences or passages were removed from the story.

Do you recall any interesting experiences from your past? Do you have relatives who said or did odd things? How did you react? Think of a time when something unusual happened in your family just because one person acted in a certain way. Brainstorm and share with your group these unique family situations. Then write about a specific event. If you need a starter, use the following prompt:

"When _____ came to visit, _____."
            (*a relative*)   (*the event that happened*)

You may add extra fictional things if you like.

Check Yourself

Read what you wrote. Did you follow the guidelines for ideas and content? What happens if the story doesn't stay focused on the topic? Did you use relevant details? Have you included too much unnecessary information?

Challenge Yourself

Think of an exciting adventure you would like to have. Draw a picture (you may use "string bean" type figures, or stick figures) showing a character doing an extreme sports activity (e.g., bungee jumping, rock climbing, surfing, stunt riding). Write a story about the character's (your) adventure. If time permits, present the story to your small group or class, using puppets or props and costumes.

My Notes

_____   _____

_____   _____

_____   _____

_____   _____

Obstacles on the Trail

Tip from the Coach

Personal insight makes writing effective.

Equipment

- colored pencils
- Oops! Watch Out for that Rock! graphic organizer, page 16

Trait Development

You may encounter unexpected rocks, logs, roots, and other obstacles along the trail, things you do not fully understand. If the descent is too steep, it can be downright frightening. Close your eyes and think about some of your own obstacles and fears; they may even be specifically related to writing. Give them form, shape, color. In a story setting, these obstacles and fears give personality to the characters. Name the "stones" you stumble over as you ride. Use the graphic organizer (Oops! Watch Out for that Rock!) on page 16 to draw, label, and color your stones and other obstacles. You may wish to white-out the "year line" on the graphic. It is used when the graphic is used with page 44. This page can serve as an illustration for a story; use the content to write a story about obstacles or fears you have overcome. As you write, consider each of the senses. What do you see? hear? Are certain smells or tastes associated with this experience? What do you feel? If time permits, rewrite your story in third person. Does the main character seem like a real person to you?

Check Yourself

How did considering things you are afraid of give you any new insights or understanding to bring to your writing?

Read the list on page 9, describing the qualities of the ideas-and-content trait; then, read your story again. Which characteristics of the trait does your writing contain? How are they effective?

My Notes

_____   _____

_____   _____

_____   _____

_____   _____

_____   _____

_____   _____

_____   _____

_____   _____

Oops! Watch Out for That Rock!

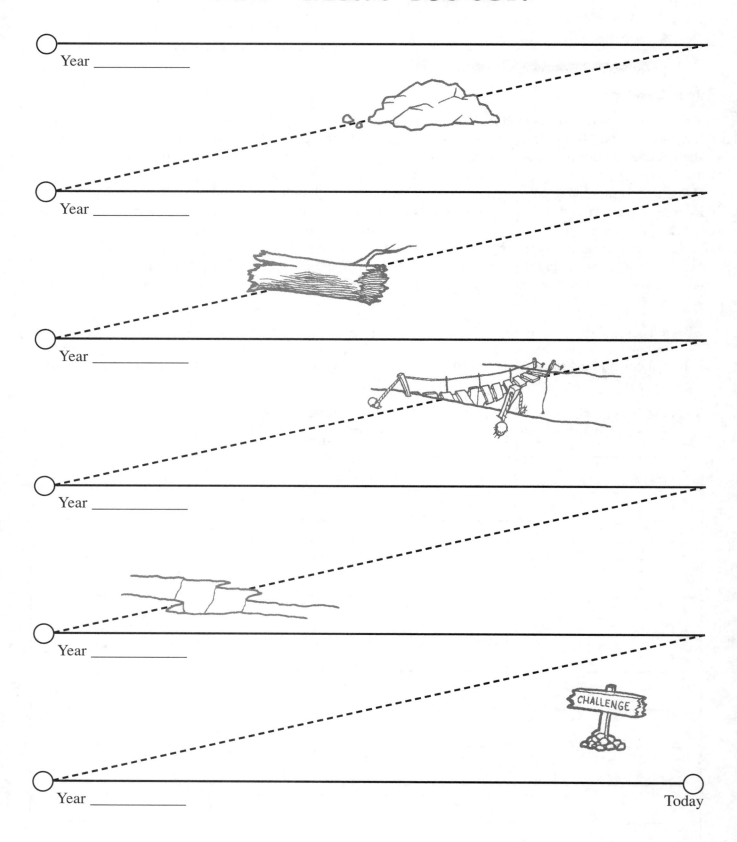

Year _____

Year _____

Year _____

Year _____

Year _____

Year _____

Today

Examine the Trail

Tip from the Coach

Successful rides are based on previous knowledge and experience.

Equipment

- Oops, Watch Out for that Rock! time line, page 16
- colored pencils

Trait Development

You may choose to ride a particular trail or race based on information you already have. Perhaps you have not ridden this trail before, but you already know something about mountain biking. You have planned this ride based on previous experience. Consider the content of your life and how it can help you on your present journey in writing.

The line on page 16 represents your life to date. Mark main events on this time line of your life. Include your birth, when you started school, etc. Use a different color and write in when special people came into your life or crossed your path. Who are these people (e.g., friends, teachers, coaches)? Why are they special to you? Mark those times when something sad happened with a third color. Use another color to write in the good times and special events (birthdays, special vacations, etc.). Finally, write in specific things you have learned (e.g., how to ride a bike).

Choose one event from your story map to write about. Begin with a "free writing" exercise. For a set amount of time (e.g., ten minutes) keep writing, stay silent, and don't stop to correct spelling. Continue to work on your story as time allows. If possible, write a second paragraph or story based on another experience from your story map. Or, rewrite the first story experience from a different perspective or point of view. Save your story map to use in later exercises.

Check Yourself

How did recalling your experiences help you construct a story based on what you know? How could you build upon this experience to write more of the story? How is this exercise an effective strategy to use in writing?

* This activity is based on an exercise used by Robert Benson in his retreat, "The Life of Prayer and the Art of Writing." Used by permission. (1999)

My Notes

_____   _____

_____   _____

_____   _____

_____   _____

_____   _____

_____   _____

Word Choice Trait

As basketball has gained popularity, we see people playing the game just about anywhere, from neighborhood games to ones on regulation courts. We also see words everywhere. What makes some words more effective than others? What makes using one word a better choice than another? Strong, visual words help an author present an image to the reader. It is important to find the right word to convey the intended meaning, to use accurate, precise words. The basketball player learns to make specific types of shots, each one with a unique visual presentation. A player will choose which shot to use in a given situation. Accurate shooting scores points for the team. In the same way, action verbs and words with energy keep a story moving. Basketball is a high energy sport, requiring players to develop action skills by practicing drills and learning ball control. The student writer learns effective word choice through practice and familiarity with the language. The words an author chooses may be long or fancy; but he or she must also be able to use words that are short, natural, and specific. Just as each basketball player develops his or her own style in the game, the successful writer will find the words and style that fit him or her and the situation in the story.

The way an author uses words can determine how effective a piece of writing is. Writers create pictures with words, and using words in new ways can expand the perspective of both the author and the reader. The sounds of words, whether read silently or aloud, add to the meaning as well.

The first two lessons in this section focus on identifying effective words. Students will organize a list of weak words and strong words. Students will also read poetry and other literature samples to become familiar with words that exhibit qualities of the word-choice trait. The third activity is based on an exercise developed by Susan G. Wooldridge. (*poemcrazy* by Susan G. Wooldridge, Clarkson Potter, 1996, pages 12–18.) In this lesson and the next, students are encouraged to use words to describe things in new and different ways to expand their perspective. Students will engage in an art project for the fourth lesson. For this activity, you will need a supply of age-appropriate old magazines. In the final lesson, students will create a promotional advertisement for their favorite basketball star or for a product that player might endorse. You may wish to create a few samples for students. You may wish to bind student advertisements into a class magazine and add other related writing assignments as well. Through these activities, students will begin to compile a list of their favorite words; this list can become a resource to use in subsequent lessons and writing assignments.

Word Choice

(to the student)

Basketball. On the neighborhood playground or on a regulation court, basketball players use a variety of specific shots to score a goal. What makes one throw result in a beautiful shot and another result in a foul or violation? A successful play catches your attention. The accuracy and precision of the winning shot leaves a vivid picture in your mind. Basketball players need not use fancy or exaggerated moves, as long as they accomplish their purpose of scoring points for their team.

A basketball player can choose specific shots and skills to use when playing a game. Similarly, the writer has many words available from which to choose. The way an author uses words can make a difference in how interesting it is to read a piece of writing. Effective word choice means using words that help the reader understand what the author is writing. Writers create pictures with words; as in basketball, you will want to choose words with strong visual imagery. Similarly, a basketball coach gives the players visual diagrams illustrating the plays the team will use during the game. Game plans may be modified based on individual team members' playing styles; each team reflects a particular playing style. Find a style of writing that fits, and use words which are natural for you. Interesting writing uses accurate, precise words in just the right way. Each player on a basketball team plays a certain position with a specific role. In your writing, choose precise words that fulfill a specific purpose. Allow your words to work together for you, just as players on a team work together. Basketball is a high-energy game of action. Use active verbs, words with energy, words that add meaning just by the way they sound. Allow words to expand your perspective as well as that of your reader.

Use Effective Word Choice

- Choose words that give strong visual imagery.
- Use words that are accurate and precise.
- Use action verbs that give your writing energy.
- Use words that sound natural.
- Listen to how the words sound.

Shots That Make the Basket . . . and Those That Don't

Tip from the Coach

Some words are more effective than others.

Equipment

- thesaurus, dictionary, and/or other resources in which to find words

Trait Development

What makes a shot a basket? or a violation? Which words should be on a writer's list of great shots? Which words can be viewed as violations in a writer's work? Under Word Violations below, write some words that are weak, too common or general, passive, or used repeatedly. You may have specific words you personally tend to overuse or misuse. Add these words to your list, too.

Use the thesaurus and other resources to go on a word hunt. Collect words you feel are "great shots," that fit the characteristics of the word-choice trait. Choose words that will catch the attention of your reader and make him or her want to read your writing. Write these words under the section titled Great Shots. The sample words will get you started.

Word Violations		Great Shots	
• cool • awesome • nice		• ruthless • ancient • flexible	

Check Yourself

Were you able to create a realistic, practical list of words that hinder you in your writing? How do you think eliminating, or at least reducing, the use of these words will strengthen your writing? What makes the words under "Great Shots" so vivid? Add words you especially like to your notebook.

My Notes

Counting Points

Tip from the Coach

Become aware of how authors use words that fit the characteristics of the word-choice trait.

Equipment

- poetry samples
- other literature samples, picture book: George, Jean Craighead. *Cliff Hanger*. HarperCollins, 2002.

Trait Development

Read the poetry samples below. As you read, notice words that exhibit characteristics of the word-choice trait. Look for specific nouns, action verbs, visual adjectives, and intriguing words with sounds that catch your attention. Find words or phrases that add visual imagery. Add these words to the Great Shots section of page 20. Do the same with any available literature samples. Add any words to your writing notebook that you feel will be especially helpful to you.

Visualize a scene from an exciting basketball game or other sporting event. Create a mental picture of an athlete's (maybe the athlete is you!) winning moment or challenge. Consider how you will describe this event—the sights, sounds, smells, tastes, touch, and feelings. What words will you use to convey action? Write a poem on another sheet of paper, using these words to portray your mental image on paper.

Check Yourself

How did reading the literature samples increase your awareness of word use in writing? Do you agree with the author's choice of words? What words would you use instead of, or in addition to, those the author chose?

Go back and read your poem again. How did the words you chose add to or detract from the picture you tried to create? Can you place yourself in the scene and experience it with all of your senses?

Bounce, bounce.

Slow motion.

Check

toes snug to the line

bounce

bend, up

the ball sails through the air

Swish.

Perfect shot.

—Tracie Heskett

He glances,

bounce-passes the ball

silent teammates

work down court

a careful dance

past guards

to the rim.

—Tracie Heskett

A Game Plan for Effective Writing

Tip from the Coach

Using words in new ways expands perspective.

Equipment

- dictionary, thesaurus, other word resources
- index cards

Trait Development

It's time to focus on making a basket. Set aside those words which hinder you in your writing. Continue to try new ways to practice using words you have not seen or used before. One way authors counter the tendency to use ineffective words is to collect new words.

Think about some of your favorite words. Why are they your favorites? What do you like about these words? Do these words catch your attention with movement or the way they sound? Do they give you a strong visual image? Add your favorite words to your writing journal; browse through a dictionary or thesaurus to collect more words.

Choose about ten words from your list and write one word on each blank index card. Use the cards to label random objects around the room. Cards may be propped up next to the object, (e.g., a globe) or taped to it (if permissible). The labels won't make sense! If you find you are trying to make it logical, close your eyes and place the cards randomly around the room. Go around the room, add the object names to the cards, and read your labels—e.g., "peach Kleenex," "sparkle door," "ridge table," or a "pool of paper."

Poetry expresses different perspectives. Changing the way you view things can be similar to coloring outside the lines or "stepping outside the box." Write a poem about a new way you see something around you. Include some of the word combinations you just discovered or other words and word phrases from your word lists.

Check Yourself

How did the labels change the way you saw things? What do the "new" labels say to you? How can you use these new words and phrases more effectively in your writing?

* This exercise is used with permission from Susan G. Wooldridge, November 1999.

My Notes

_____   _____

_____   _____

_____   _____

_____   _____

_____   _____

Photo Album

Equipment

- old magazines
- scratch paper and a piece of 9" x 12" (23 cm x 30 cm) construction paper or tagboard (larger if desired)
- scissors, glue

Trait Development

"A picture is worth a thousand words." What does that quotation say to you? What do you think of when you hear the phrase "word picture"?

A word collage contains words that communicate thoughts and feelings to another person. You will create a picture with words instead of drawings.

Think of an idea or concept (e.g., peace, family, conflict) that you would like to express. First, write that one-word idea or concept at the top of a piece of scratch paper. This is what your word picture will describe. List words to tell about your idea and then look through the magazines to find letters and/or words to portray your idea. Do not use your original word elsewhere in your collage. Attempt to connect words in unusual ways, but also try to choose effective words so others will be able to guess your original idea. Glue the letters and/or words you find to the piece of construction paper.

If time permits, ask someone else to guess what idea they think you are trying to portray in your collage. You may also wish to write a story based on your word collage.

Check Yourself

Step back from your collage for a minute. Look at the entire picture. How do the words you used convey your message? What specific words did you choose and why did you include those words? What made these words effective or ineffective?

Were others able to guess the idea you wanted to portray? How do you think words can create a picture?

My Notes

_____   _____

_____   _____

_____   _____

_____   _____

_____   _____

_____   _____

Starring . . .

Tip from the Coach

You can use words in new and different ways to persuade others.

Equipment

- pages 25 and 26, "The Greatest . . ."
- construction paper or tagboard
- markers, sample advertisements, and product descriptions (optional)

Trait Development

In this exercise, you will create a promotional piece for your favorite basketball or other sports figure. Or, you may choose to design an advertisement for a product that person might endorse (e.g., shoes, soft drinks). Remember as you work through this activity to use words that exhibit characteristics of the word-choice trait—specifically, precise words that describe accurately, active verbs, high-energy language, and words that sound natural or catch the reader's attention by the way they sound.

Before you begin to design your advertisement, you may want to look at some samples if available. How does the advertisement catch your attention? How are words used effectively to promote the item for sale? What specific words, details, reasons, evidence, examples, and/or arguments do the authors use to convince the reader to buy their product?

Create a promotion or advertisement using the graphic organizers on pages 25 and 26, "The Greatest . . ." (e.g., basketball player, coach, high energy bar, etc.). Complete each section of the work sheets as they pertain to your person or product. Remember to use specific and descriptive words that have qualities of strong word choice. After you have completed the work sheet, design a poster using your ideas.

Check Yourself

If time allows, share your advertisement with your class. Ask other students if they can tell what person or product you are trying to advertise. Ask why they would or would not want to buy this product. Have the class identify the words you used that exhibit characteristics of the word-choice trait.

My Notes

_____   _____

_____   _____

_____   _____

_____   _____

_____   _____

_____   _____

_____   _____

The Greatest . . .

Name of Person

_____

Attributes of Person

_____

_____

_____

Outstanding Accomplishments

_____

_____

_____

How is your person special?

_____

_____

_____

Why should someone attend a sporting event to watch this person?

_____

_____

_____

How much does it cost to attend a sporting event? How can the spectator purchase tickets?

_____

_____

_____

What is the location of the sporting event? What are the directions to get there?

_____

_____

_____

Design the logo or illustration for the sporting event starring your person.

The Greatest . . . *(cont.)*

Name of Product

_____

Features of Product

_____

_____

_____

Outstanding Qualities

_____

_____

_____

How is your product unique?

_____

_____

_____

Why should someone buy this product?

_____

_____

_____

How much does the product cost? How can someone buy or order the product?

_____

_____

_____

Design the logo or illustration for the product.

Fluency Trait

This series of lessons uses swimming to illustrate the characteristics of the fluency trait. Swimming traditionally has served several purposes, including escape, relief, and enjoyment. Swimmers may use a combination of strokes such as crawl, backstroke, and breast stroke. A swimmer chooses which stroke to use based on one's mood and purpose. Children play in water at an early age, and most people continue to find being in water relaxing. Swimming is rhythmic, the athletes appearing to glide smoothly through the water. The mood of a swimmer adjusts to circumstances. When competing, the athlete must use strategy. A swimmer may choose to use different strokes, depending on the situation—e.g., a crawl stroke for speed in a race or a breast stroke for leisurely situations. The athlete does not expend any more energy than necessary or waste any movements; he or she will use a stroke based on efficiency. The swimmer needs an awareness of competitors, knowing whether they start fast or swim steadily with a burst of speed at the end of the race. He or she needs to consider the question, "what if . . .?" When not racing, those who swim often do so for pure enjoyment, splashing and playing in the water.

Fluent writing has many of these same characteristics. The author plays with language, using a variety of word patterns to convey the message. Fluent writing incorporates natural rhythm and flow. It passes the read-aloud test. The fluent author uses clear sentences that make sense, with no extra words. Sentence length and structure are varied. The author asks the question "what if . . .?" and uses smooth transitions so that ideas begin purposefully and connect with each other.

Students begin this series of lessons by completing a word association activity using a graphic organizer. In the next exercise, they read a passage from a literature selection. You may wish to have them read aloud with a partner; fluency often can be detected as words are read aloud. Students are then encouraged to engage in a process of thinking, asking and answering the question "What if . . . ?" Students continue to build a sense of rhythm and natural flow by writing while listening to music. For this exercise, you will need an instrumental selection approximately ten minutes in length and a CD or tape player. You may also find it helpful to make poetry samples available to students. In the fourth lesson, students participate in a group activity to write mixed-up silly stories. Finally, they will bring it all back together by writing a complete story from start to finish, using as many qualities of the fluency trait as possible.

Fluency

(to the student)

People of all ages enjoy playing in water. Lakes, creeks, rivers, waterfalls, and oceans beckon to us. Each has its own mood, rhythm, and movement. Over time, swimming has met many purposes, and has developed as a sport that encompasses many different activities. Originally, people swam to escape danger, catch food, find relief from the heat of the sun, or for pure enjoyment. A swimmer chooses a stroke to meet his or her needs at that moment; each stroke has movements that are efficient for a certain purpose. For example, the sidestroke is used for power, the crawl stroke gives speed and efficiency, the backstroke conserves energy, and the breaststroke is a restful, relaxing stroke.

Fluent writing also has its own natural rhythm and flow. A fluent writer uses variety in his or her sentence length and structure. You will want to choose words and phrases to suit your purposes. As you develop fluency in your writing, you will learn to play with language, word patterns, and rhythm. Not everyone hears the same rhythm; find your own. At the same time, you will want to use clear sentences that make sense, with no extra words. Your ideas will begin purposefully and connect with each other. If your writing exhibits characteristics of the fluency trait, it will pass the "read-aloud test," sounding natural as you or another person reads your writing aloud. More than one of the exercises in this section uses the technique of "free writing," which means you will write for a set period of time, without stopping or self-editing.

Exhibit the Characteristics of Fluency

- using varied sentence length and structure
- developing a natural rhythm and flow
- using a process of thinking (e.g., ask the question, "What if . . . ?")
- using different word patterns
- playing with language
- using clear sentences that make sense
- developing ideas that begin purposefully and connect to one another
- using words to match the mood
- using no extra words
- passing the read-aloud test

Splashing in Fluency

Equipment

• writing materials
• Playing in the Water graphic organizer

Trait Development

Think about synchronized swimming, playing with rhythm, patterns, reflecting different moods. Familiarize yourself with the characteristics of the fluency trait listed on page 28.

Use the graphic organizer below, Playing in the Water, to create a waterfall or cascade of words. To begin, choose a word from your word list or other resource. Write it at the top of the waterfall. "Free write," using word association to complete the rest of the page: write the first word or phrase that comes to your mind when you say your beginning word, then write the next, etc. Try to connect with the picture you see in your mind. Choose a group of words or related ideas. Write a poem or story scene using the words, ideas, and concepts you generated.

If you have time, work with a partner to list words relating to a specific topic—e.g., swimming or diving. You may want to play with word patterns or make up some nonsense words and list those as well.

Check Yourself

What common theme do you see in the words and phrases you wrote? What connections did you find? Did your thoughts and ideas flow smoothly in a logical sequence?

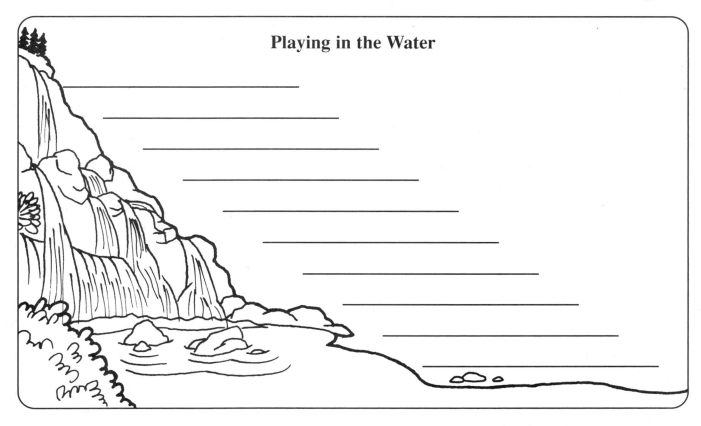

Playing in the Water

What If . . . ?

> **Tip from the Coach**
>
> An author must balance many characteristics in his or her writing.

Equipment

- a literature sample you feel flows especially well, or one of the titles suggested below.
- picture book: *Swim the Silver Sea, Joshie Otter* by Nancy White Carlstrom. Philomel Books, 1993. *Otter on His Own: The Story of a Sea Otter* by Doe Boyle. Soundprints, 1995.
- chapter book: *Shark Beneath the Reef* by Jean Craighead George. HarperTrophy, 1989.

Trait Development

(Your teacher may have you complete this exercise with a partner.)

Read a story of your choice that you feel has strong rhythm. After you finish reading, go back and notice the way the author used sentence structure and rhythm. How does the story flow? Also notice word patterns. How does the author play with language? Do the sentences make sense? Study the sentence structure in the story. How do the sentences vary in length? Do they all begin in the same way? How has the author used sentence variety to add interest for the reader?

Look for connections between ideas. What purposes do you see in the story? Are the transitions smooth? Compare the literature sample to your writing from the previous exercise. What can you learn from this author's writing?

Ask yourself, "What if . . . ?" What if the characters in the story had done some things differently? What if some events in the story had not happened? What if the story had ended in another way? Write some "What if . . . ?" questions related to the story you read. Use the technique of "free writing" to write your own ending to the story, using one of your questions as a story starter.

If possible, you and your partner may wish to read a picture book aloud to younger students. If you choose this activity, practice reading the story first, focusing on the rhythm and flow of the author's words.

Check Yourself

What elements of fluency were present in the story you read? How did the story flow; how did the action move forward with purpose? Which elements of fluency were you able to incorporate in your writing? Were you able to experiment with word patterns and play with language? Review how the author used rhythm, a variety of sentence structures, word patterns, and playing with language to tell a story.

> **My Notes**
>
> _____   _____
>
> _____   _____
>
> _____   _____
>
> _____   _____
>
> _____   _____

Dance in the Water

Equipment

- instrumental music selection, at least ten minutes in length
- CD or tape player
- poetry selections

Trait Development

Mentally picture the rhythms of the ocean, a waterfall, or a river. Can you hear the music in the waves, in the splashes as you swim? An ocean, creek, or lake has more than a steady beat; each changes yet remains the same.

Think of rhythm as more than rhyme or a steady beat, and tap out a rhythm pattern on your desk with your hands or fingers. (If you don't feel comfortable making up a rhythm, beat out the rhythm of a song you know.) Think about the loud and soft beats, the accents, how the sound flows.

Read one or two of your favorite poems aloud, if available. Compare the sound of the spoken words with the rhythm pattern you tapped out. How does human speech sound like music? What do talking and singing or talking and music have in common?

Listen to the instrumental music selection. While you are listening, write. Write for at least ten minutes without stopping or self-editing. Use the music to its full advantage; if it reminds you of a certain place, try to imagine how the scene would look. If the rhythm makes you think of action, write about what is happening. After the time is up, go back and read your work aloud quietly to yourself. Try to tap out the rhythm of the words as you read.

Check Yourself

Did you find it easy or difficult to write while listening to music? Why? How did the music help you write fluently? How did this exercise help you put natural rhythm and flow into your writing?

My Notes

_____   _____
_____   _____
_____   _____
_____   _____
_____   _____
_____   _____
_____   _____
_____   _____

Just Splashing Around

Tip from the Coach

Work with others to develop a sense of fun and pattern in your writing.

Equipment

- story starters
- writing materials

Trait Development

(Your teacher may have you work with a small group to complete this exercise.)

Read the story starter your teacher gives you. Consider the questions "What if . . . ?" and "What happens next?" Write two follow-up sentences to come after the story starter. Fold the paper over so your writing does not show. Pass the paper to the next person in your group. As each person passes his or her paper around, you will receive another story. Write two more sentences for that story, without reading what the previous person wrote. Continue writing sentences and passing the stories around until you have received your original story starter back. Unfold the papers and read the silly stories to each other.

Check Yourself

Discuss with others in your group how these mixed-up stories do or do not exhibit characteristics of the fluency trait. What factors affected the fluency? How were these stories easier or harder to understand?

My Notes

_____   _____

_____   _____

_____   _____

_____   _____

_____   _____

_____   _____

_____   _____

_____   _____

_____   _____

_____   _____

Just Splashing Around (cont.)

Story Starter #1

Robert lay in bed staring at the water stain on the ceiling right over his head. The stain was oddly shaped, and he often imagined it was a map of a different country . . .

Story Starter #2

"Look!" John pointed a finger at the light flickering through the trees beyond the cabin window. Caleb didn't answer. Instead, he covered his head with his sleeping bag . . .

Story Starter #3

Once, very long ago, an old man lived in the remains of a castle. He could not speak, but those who lived in the countryside around knew of his helpfulness . . .

Story Starter #4

"I'm running away and never coming back!" Tara stomped her feet and ran outside. She slammed the door behind her . . .

Story Starter #5

Silently, I walked up to the edge of the crowd. The people were intent, watching some activity on the lake shore. I stood on my toes and tried to see over the heads of those standing in front of me . . .

Different Strokes

Tip from the Coach

The author conveys a mood not only through the words he chooses, but also through his use of language, rhythm, and sentence structure.

Equipment

- pictures
- index cards

Trait Development

Study the pictures on page 35 carefully. Label five index cards: *character*, *setting-place*, *setting-time*, *mood*, and *conflict*. Remember that story conflict involves interesting action and/or a problem the main character must solve. Make notes on each card, just a few words describing what each picture conveys to you. Use the pictures and note cards to write a complete story. As you begin to write, determine how you will develop reader interest and establish the situation and plot. What point of view will you use? How will you use dialogue in your story? What elements of fluency can you incorporate into your story to make it flow naturally?

If possible, read some of your classmates' stories or listen as they read their stories aloud. Could you determine the setting, mood, and conflict of their stories? How did their writing exhibit characteristics of the fluency trait?

Check Yourself

Which aspects of fluency did you find easy to incorporate into your own story? Which characteristics are more difficult for you? How does your story read more naturally, smoothly, fluently, than the mixed-up stories in the previous exercise?

My Notes

_____   _____
_____   _____
_____   _____
_____   _____
_____   _____
_____   _____
_____   _____
_____   _____
_____   _____

Different Strokes *(cont.)*

Voice Trait

Each snowboarder's style reflects his or her "voice"—a unique personality that comes through the riding. On the snow, the rider may participate in a variety of activities, including racing, freestyle riding, jumping, riding off-trail, and extreme competitions. Snowboarding is a sport that allows the athlete self-discovery and freedom of expression. Snowboarders are encouraged to know their capabilities and stay within their limits when trying new runs or tricks.

Writing that has strong "voice" is sincere, honest, and focused on the audience, while at the same time reflecting the author's own personality. The reader can sense a real person behind the words. To develop a unique voice, an author must know himself or herself as a writer and then write out of that knowledge. Writers develop their voice by writing with confidence and bringing the topic to life. Just as each snowboarder has a unique way of expressing himself or herself while performing for the crowd, a writer will write specifically to the reader. A writer who uses strong voice will be himself or herself without trying to exaggerate or impress the reader beyond his or her abilities. The writing will come from the author's thoughts, feelings, and who he or she is as a person.

Students will begin learning about voice by participating in a listening activity. They will write a response using qualities of the voice trait. Students will also be asked to read work by anonymous authors and then try to guess what kind of person wrote the piece. (*When photocopying page 41 for student use, you will need to fold over the bottom section so students won't have the answers.*) You may want to ask your students to type a short paragraph; when you receive the student papers, remove the names and redistribute the paragraphs to the class. Have students try to guess which one of their classmates wrote the piece. In the next activity, students will write another paragraph or two, trying to use another specific person's voice. You may wish to tie this in with a literature selection and/or an author study, having students write as if they were that author. Students will need their life story-map, Oops! Watch Out for that Rock! from Ideas and Content, page 16 for the fourth exercise. In the final lesson students continue to develop their voice by writing a business letter of request. You may need to teach the basic format of a business letter if it has not already been introduced.

Voice

(to the student)

Snowboarding is a popular sport with young people. It allows for self-discovery and freedom of expression. One of the first things a snowboarder learns is to control the board. You should know yourself and your abilities before you try anything new on the slopes. Snowboarding is a sport that requires careful attention to safety, rules, and details. Stay in control, maintain an awareness of other riders, pay attention to your surroundings, be honest, sincere, and confident, develop your own style, and you will enjoy snowboarding to the fullest.

If your writing has qualities of strong voice, your personality will come through in your writing. Bring your writing to life with energy and sincerity. You will want to focus on your reader, writing and talking directly to him or her. Make your writing sound as if your reader is there with you. The reader will recognize a real person behind your words. A piece with voice has natural rhythm, just as there is a rhythm to snowboarding. Write honestly and with confidence. Write from your own self-knowledge, polishing your unique style.

Write with Your Own Unique Voice

- Make a piece sound like a particular person wrote it.

- Allow your personality to come through in the writing.

- Use natural rhythm.

- Hook your reader; call attention to the writing.

- Convey honesty and self-knowledge.

- Write to your reader.

- Bring your topic to life.

- Give your writing personality, and let the reader sense the real person behind the words.

© *Teacher Created Materials, Inc.*   37   *#3359 Using the Traits of Good Writing*

The Sounds of the Slopes

Tip from the Coach

Listen to the world around you.

Equipment

- writing notebook
- pen or pencil

Trait Development

Listen. Listen to yourself and to others. Take your writing notebook or this page outside. Sit silently and listen to the sounds around you. What do you hear? If possible, you may also want to listen at night or in a forest or in the snow. Write about what you hear. Try writing in different forms: narrative, descriptive, poetry, perhaps a letter. Think of a time in your life when you experienced a challenge or a problem. Write about how you faced the challenge and overcame the obstacle or problem.

Check Yourself

What sounds did you hear? When you read back over your writing, how does your personality come through? How does the writing sound like a real person? Is your writing sincere?

My Notes

Whose Style?

Tip from the Coach

An author's personality comes through his or her writing. Learn to identify voice.

Equipment

- sample paragraphs on pages 40 and 41, Who Is That?
- writing materials

Trait Development

You have listened and identified specific sounds. In this exercise, you will try to determine an author's personality or voice, by reading his or her writing. If a piece has a particularly strong voice, you might be able to identify what type of person wrote it.

Read through the samples on pages 40 and 41, Who Is That? For each paragraph, write down your thoughts as to the identity of the author. Who do you think wrote the piece—a male or female? How old is the person? What do you think this person does for a living? What qualities of the writing make it sound as if a real person is talking?

Make up an identity for a person: decide whether the person is male or female, his or her age, what job the person has, and one other fact. Write a paragraph as if you were that person.

Check Yourself

Could you identify the personalities of the authors? What specific qualities in their writing helped or hindered you in making your judgments?

When you wrote a sample paragraph, did it sound like your "made-up person" wrote it, or did your own voice come through? Ask a classmate to read your sample paragraph, and then ask him or her whether it sounds like you or the "made-up person."

My Notes

_____ _____

_____ _____

_____ _____

_____ _____

_____ _____

_____ _____

_____ _____

_____ _____

Who Is That?

Sample Paragraph #1

"No remarkable plays until nearly game's end. Suddenly she spins off hits by both opponents and DIVES after the black tailback scooting through the huge hole. Catching him at the knees, she's dragged three or four yards and then gets shaken off . . . just in time for her teammates to jump the carrier. Mary's face is ashen."

Sample Paragraph #2

Once upon a time there was a person with a green truck with blue seats and blue driver and blue pedals. He even had a blue seatbelt. He also had a blue siren. The siren would have meant he had a giant engine so he could go in rough fields. He could also be a snowplow. One day it was snowy so he had to put out his snowplow. Then before he pushed out snow he found a whole bunch of signs that said No cars coming in here or no snow plows because the kids want to play in the snow and make snow men. He was happy because he wanted to play in the snow, so he drove his snowplow back to his home. It was so snowy that the snow got from the ground to the top of the deck.

Sample Paragraph #3

I think that snowboarding is a great sport for both the athletic and those who aren't so athletically inclined, but just like to have fun. Snowboarding is foreign to many people who live in very dry areas of the country and in low elevations far away from the mountains. It's sad that they have to be deprived of this exciting activity that is such a common practice of those who live in cooler areas of the country. The first thing that comes into my head concerning snowboarding is the challenge of turning corners, which is what causes a lot of people injuries and fear. As you're at the top of a hill and you begin going down it, you might begin to feel stable and as though you've got this sport under control, and then suddenly you come to a curve and you lose all the control you thought you once had and land flat on your rear in the cool snow. It might hurt a bit at first, but once you get back onto your feet, you feel the rush of adrenaline come back and prepare to do it all over again. That is just a part of what makes snowboarding such a fabulous sport and why it has captured the time and attention of so many people.

Who Is That? *(cont.)*

Sample Paragraph #4

He took a deep breath. He was ready. The air was fresh, and so was the snow. His snowboard was slightly cocked to the right, to give him an angled start. He took a final breath and pushed off. The slope was steep, and his speed fast. He had a good chance of breaking his old record. Jeff smiled as his speed increased. He loved the exhilaration and fresh air. He laughed aloud, thinking. Was it only a month ago that he started this sport? He was already prepared for the contest in a month or so. Because of this he was ready for the sharp turn ahead. His laughter died on his lips as he rounded the turn. Up ahead was a sheer drop off that had not been there days ago. A slide? Not likely. He turned quickly and steered off the path. Jeff was still going about 30 mph and he had to stop. As he crashed through the bushes, he failed to notice the tree up ahead. He hit it at 20 mph, and everything went black.

Sample Paragraph #5

Swimming is fun. I like going swimming with my friends and family. Sometimes we get to stay in the pool for 4 or 5 hours. I like swimming! I bring my snorkel and goggles in it too. Boy, I'm spoiled. O yeah, I'm going to the beach for my sister's birthday in June. Boy, I like it. You should too!

Paragraphs Used by Permission of Original Authors

Sample Paragraph #1   Dennis Blackwell, male, age 46

Sample Paragraph #2   Brian Mabry, male, age 6

Sample Paragraph #3   Jessica Petty, female, age 21, small business owner

Sample Paragraph #4   Kenneth Mabry, male, age 14

Sample Paragraph #5   Geneva Ford, female, age 8

The Style and Voices of . . .

Tip from the Coach

Practice writing in a specific person's voice.

Equipment

- literature selection
- The Style and Voices of . . . , page 43.

Trait Development

How do you think a particular person's style on a snowboard will look? Will a guy have a different style than a girl? Will a grownup ride differently than a teen? Think about individual styles.

Read the story passage your teacher provides silently, observing any characteristics of the voice trait. Read it again, aloud, to really "hear" the author's "voice." Write about four scenes from the story. Choose scenes that illustrate a particular aspect of the voice trait. How might the characters talk in the scene? What would they talk about? What language would they use? What other characters might have been included in the story?

Fill in the conversation balloons on page 43 with phrases the characters you selected might say. Or write in the balloons how a particular scene demonstrates voice—e.g., you could write, "this shows honesty," or "the author writes to the reader when he says . . . ," or "it sounds like a particular person wrote this piece." Have fun with this, don't struggle, and enjoy yourself.

If you have time, write the next segment of the story. Try to see the characters from the author's perspective. What would the characters say? What words would they use?

Check Yourself

In the story you read, how did it seem like a real person was telling the story? What did the author say that made it feel like he or she was talking directly to you, the reader? What are some ways you could begin to use the qualities of the voice trait in your own writing?

My Notes

_____   _____

_____   _____

_____   _____

_____   _____

_____   _____

_____   _____

_____   _____

The Style and Voices of . . . *(cont.)*

Directions: Fill in the conversation balloons with phrases the characters you selected might say. Or write in the balloons how a particular scene demonstrates voice as a trait of good writing.

_____
_____
_____
_____
_____
_____

(Character or Scene)

_____
_____
_____
_____
_____
_____

(Character or Scene)

_____
_____
_____
_____
_____
_____

(Character or Scene)

_____
_____
_____
_____
_____
_____

(Character or Scene)

Developing My Own Style

Equipment

- Oops! Watch Out for That Rock! (page 16), from Ideas and Content
- colored pencils

Trait Development

Think back over your life, the new skills you have learned, challenges and obstacles you have faced. In this exercise, you will continue to chart out the course of your life, the smooth runs, the jumps, the insight you have gained.

Lay your Obstacles on the Trail page out before you. Review the characteristics of the voice trait. How do you hear your own voice? When do you hear it? Where? Think about those times when you feel the most like yourself, the most comfortable with yourself.

Use a color you have not yet used and mark the times and/or events when you have been able to rest, relax, be yourself, have fun. Also mark times (with the same color or a different color, it does not matter) when you felt the most like yourself. Note the circumstances surrounding those times.

Use a different color to mark times when something sad happened. Write on your page what you learned from the experience and/or how you were able to help someone else out of that experience.

Write a few paragraphs about one of the events from your life. Try to make your voice come through in your writing. Do you know yourself well enough to write from your own life?

Check Yourself

If possible, have someone else read your writing. How would this person know you wrote it? How does your personality come through your writing? Have you written honestly and sincerely about the experience you chose from your life? What characteristics of the voice trait were you able to use successfully?

My Notes

_____   _____

_____   _____

_____   _____

_____   _____

_____   _____

_____   _____

Snowboarding for Everyone

Equipment
- writing notebook
- pen or pencil

Trait Development

Snowboarders maintain an awareness of their audience, but more than that, they remain focused for their entire run. Effective writing should focus on the reader, yet remain honest and sincere, reflecting the writer's personality. Just as there are different skills and purposes in snowboarding, such as racing, jumping, off-trail riding, and extreme competition, you will also write in various ways, depending on your audience.

Consider how characteristics of the voice trait might apply to writing a business letter. You will want to be yourself, not trying to exaggerate or impress the reader unnecessarily. Your writing will flow from your thoughts, feelings, and who you are as a person. You will want to bring your topic to life so your letter will catch the attention of the reader.

Think of a ski resort that does not currently allow snowboarders. Write a business letter to the resort, asking for permission to snowboard at their resort. Remember to follow some of the basic guidelines of snowboarding as you write the letter: be courteous, show your awareness of and willingness to follow the rules, show your sincerity and responsibility. Focus on your reader and write directly to that person. If you are not near a ski resort, write to another sports-related business with a specific request. You may need to check with your teacher for ideas.

Check Yourself

How did incorporating characteristics of the voice trait make the letter easier or more interesting to write? Why should the recipient read your letter? Will your letter leave a favorable impression with the reader regarding snowboarding or your other request? If you worked for the ski resort, would you read the letter you have just written? Why or why not?

My Notes

_____   _____

_____   _____

_____   _____

_____   _____

_____   _____

_____   _____

_____   _____

Organization Trait

This section uses the game of soccer as a metaphor for organizing writing. Soccer is an organized game with a logical order and sequence. Players have clear direction and a stated purpose to make the goal. The coach makes sure all players understand the game plan at the beginning of the game; successful strategy will lead the team to a satisfying conclusion at the end of the game. In like manner, the trait of organization gives the reader a clear path through written work. The writer guides the reader through the story with a clear direction and logical sequence of events. Transitions tie ideas together, and there is appropriate pacing throughout the writing; it flows smoothly. Just as the soccer coach leads his players, a writer grabs the reader's attention and provides a satisfying ending that makes the reader think.

A graphic organizer is a tool to help writers organize their writing. In soccer, each player is responsible for a certain position on the field. Each position has a specific role, which enables play to remain organized. This helps the team to control the ball and stay focused on scoring a goal. Writers also need to refer back to the main idea as they write. Just as a forward shoots directly at the goal to score, the author wants to help the reader reach the most important moment, or climax, of the story.

Students begin to find their way through the trait of organization by working their way through a maze and reviewing characteristics of the trait. They practice finding their way through someone else's writing by using a sequencing activity. In the next lesson, students examine leads and conclusions from literature. Students then check their own writing for qualities of organization by completing a graphic organizer. They will need two copies of My Game Plan, page 53. The final exercise is to plot and sequence a story and then create it.

Organization

(to the student)

You're on the soccer field. Have you ever watched or played in a soccer game in which the players did not play their positions? How difficult was it to remain focused on the goal? In such a game, each player might not be sure what to do next or how to help the team score a goal.

Soccer is an organized game with a logical order and sequence. As a writer, you are like the soccer player, coach, or referee, all of whom work together to ensure the game flows smoothly. You will write the game plan, or strategy, and then lead the reader through. You will want to make sure you have your reader's attention at the beginning of your writing. In the game of soccer, each player has a specific position with a specific role to play. Play must remain organized to score a goal. Players have a clear direction in that they have one purpose. You need to organize your writing in such a way as to lead your reader through your words. Make sure your writing has clear direction so you do not lose your reader. In organized writing, transitions tie ideas together and there is appropriate pacing; the writing flows smoothly. Soccer players must pace themselves, or they will tire before the end of the game. The game of soccer flows almost continuously, with passing and teamwork, smooth transitions, and not many time outs. In writing it is important to know where and when you are beginning and ending. Provide a satisfying conclusion that will make your reader think. Don't make it too predictable; it's okay to change direction occasionally, keep the other team thinking. Soccer is a team sport; don't leave anyone behind. When you write, you and your reader are on the journey together. Help your reader stay focused on the main idea as you write. Lead your reader through the game to the climax of the story—the most important moment of the game—when your team makes a goal, the kick that scores.

Include These Characteristics of Organization

- a path leading the reader to the main point

- a clear direction and purpose

- an attention-getting introduction

- a conclusion that makes the reader think

- a logical order and sequencing of details

- appropriate pacing

- transitions that tie ideas together

- links back to the main idea

Finding Your Way Through the Game Plan

Tip from the Coach

Familiarity with the characteristics of the organization trait will help you in your writing.

Equipment

- Finding Your Way Through the Game Plan, page 48

Trait Development

You're running toward the goal, hoping to make the kick and score the goal that wins the game. You dribble, pass, trap the ball, dribble again, moving the ball down the field. It is like running through a maze, as you shield, guard, and tackle (take the ball) other players. Complete the maze below, noting the characteristics of the organization trait as you work your way through from start to finish.

On the back of this page, design a maze for a partner. As your partner completes your maze, have him or her tell you about (or write down) the characteristics of the organization trait.

Check Yourself

Discuss with your partner how you will remember the qualities of this trait.

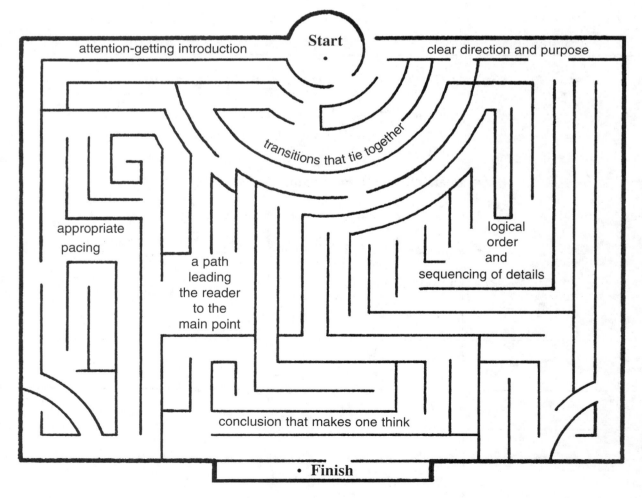

What's the Strategy?

Equipment

- one of your favorite short stories or other literature selection
- index cards or sticky notes
- picture book option: *Soccer* by Robin Russell. The Bookwright Press, 1992.

Trait Development

Consider the last soccer game you heard about, observed, or participated in. What were some of the opening moves? Were any players able to run straight to the goal, or did the other team play strong defense, keeping the offensive team constantly on guard?

Read a story or passage by one of your favorite authors or from the literature sample your teacher provides. Think about the order of events that takes place in the story. What happens at the beginning of the story? What happens at the end? Is there a satisfying conclusion? Does the story have clear direction and flow smoothly?

On index cards or sticky notes, write the main events of the story you read, one event or scene per card. Lay them out in no particular order. Does the story make sense? Now arrange them in the proper order. What is the difference? How is the story more enjoyable when arranged correctly?

Now, number the nonfiction sentences listed below in the correct order.

_____ Each team member must be aware of where other players are on the field.

_____ People around the world enjoy this fast-paced game of action.

_____ The oldest known team sport in the world is soccer.

_____ Soccer is a game of running, quick speed, clear thinking, and focusing on the goal.

_____ In the game of soccer, team members work together to control the ball and set up scoring opportunities.

_____ It is also important for each person to play his or her position.

Check Yourself

How does an author organize his or her writing? What do you notice about the beginning? the end? Which sequencing task did you find more difficult, the fiction or nonfiction? Why?

My Notes

_____   _____

_____   _____

_____   _____

_____   _____

_____

The Kickoff . . . and the Goal

Tip from the Coach

An effective lead grabs the reader's attention, and a satisfying conclusion makes him or her think.

Equipment
- writing notebook
- pen or pencil

Trait Development

At the beginning of the game, it is important that each player be in position for the kickoff. The crowd watches carefully to see which team will gain possession of the ball and take it down the field. How are you going to generate interest so the reader will want to come along with you? Throughout the game, you keep your purpose clearly in mind: to help your team score goals and win the game. How will you make sure your reader is still there with you at the end?

What is it about the first few sentences of a book that makes you want to keep reading it? How might an author get the reader's attention?

List some of your thoughts and ideas in your writing notebook.

Read the following story beginnings:

"It was almost December, and Jonas was beginning to be frightened." (*The Giver* by Lois Lowry. Dell Publishing, 1993.)

"Like silent, hungry sharks that swim in the darkness of the sea, the German submarines arrived in the middle of the night." (*The Cay* by Theodore Taylor. Avon Books, 1969.)

"I understood almost nothing about the woods until it was nearly too late." (*Woodsong* by Gary Paulsen. Aladdin Library, 2002.)

"Clarice Donners was always messing around. She said it came with the name." (*Dangerous Devices* by T. Davis Bunn. Chariot Books, 1996.)

"A sudden snow shower put an end to hockey practice." (*Many Waters* by Madeleine L'Engle. Yearling Books, 1987.)

"If you'd like a story about how I won my basketball letter and achieved fame, love, and fortune, don't read this." (*Very Far Away from Anywhere Else* by Ursula K. LeGuin. Bantam, 1982.)

How are these leads effective? Compare your list of thoughts to the authors' leads. Write some story beginnings of your own in your writing notebook.

The Kickoff . . . and the Goal *(cont.)*

What makes a satisfying conclusion? Does the author abruptly decide it is "the end" because he or she is tired of writing and/or has run out of things to say? Read the following conclusions:

"I stood there and did the human act as well as possible." (*Very Far Away from Anywhere Else* by Ursula K. LeGuin. Atheneum, 1976.)

"Behind him, across vast distances of space and time, from the place he had left, he thought he heard music too. But perhaps it was only an echo." (*The Giver* by Lois Lowry. Dell Publishing, 1993.)

"Brian tried several times to tell his father, came really close once to doing it, but in the end never said a word about the man or what he knew, the Secret." (*Hatchet* by Gary Paulsen. Aladdin Paperbacks, 1987.)

"'I'll only be gone a month,' I said. 'Maybe a little longer . . .'" (*Jaguar* by Roland Smith. Hyperion Press, 1998.)

"Because it was about time I shared my life with them. And this was a good place to start." (*Scarlet Thunder* by Sigmund Brouwer. Thomas Nelson, 1998.)

"Doug looked up at his teacher, coach, and friend and said, 'Who says everyone can't have an Olympic dream?'" (*Olympic Dream* by Matt Christopher. Little, Brown, and Co., 1996.)

How did the authors make you think? Why would you want to read more? List qualities that made these conclusions effective or ineffective. Practice writing some story endings in your notebook.

Check Yourself

Read back through your sample beginnings. Do they grab your attention? Why or why not?

Would your endings leave your reader feeling satisfied? What did you learn about writing leads and conclusions? What makes this part of writing easy or difficult?

My Notes

_____   _____

_____   _____

_____   _____

_____   _____

Here's the Plan . . .

Equipment

- My Game Plan, page 53, two copies
- your stories from previous writing exercises

Trait Development

Your team lost the game. You meet with the coach, review the game, and discuss how each half of the game went. Did each player hold position? Or did your game turn into a disorganized mess? Perhaps halfway through the game your team got tired or lost interest in the main purpose. Help your reader by pacing your writing appropriately. Keep the main idea in mind as you write. As you invite your reader to experience the game with you, you need to remove any obstacles that hinder you from reaching the goal; give your reader smooth transitions that tie ideas together. Help the reader reach the goal, the most important moment in the story.

Plot out a story using My Game Plan, page 53. Write your story beginning or lead next to the space that says "Kickoff." Next to "Purpose," tell why you want to write this story. You may not actually use what you write for purpose, but you should complete this part to help you stay focused on the main idea of your story. Write what your story is about next to "Main Idea." In every story, the main character has a problem to solve, a challenge or conflict to overcome. The next part of your story will be "Scoring the Goal," the most important moment in the story, when the character faces the conflict, problem, or meets the challenge. You may also want to write here how the problem is resolved. Write your ending next to "Conclusion." How will planning your writing make the finished story well organized so that it makes sense?

Next, complete a separate copy of the graphic organizer, using a story you wrote in a previous exercise. What, if any, missing pieces do you need to fill in? What other changes do you need to make? Rewrite your story, incorporating characteristics of the organization trait.

Check Yourself

How did using the graphic organizer help you organize your thoughts and writing? How can you use this exercise to help you pace your story, including smooth transitions?

My Notes

_____   _____

_____   _____

_____   _____

_____   _____

_____   _____

My Game Plan

It's a Classic

Equipment

- Classic Strategy, page 55
- writing materials

> **Tip from the Coach**
>
> Stories may follow one of several basic plot categories.

Trait Development

Make sure your shoes are tied, take one last drink of water, and run out onto the field. Are you ready to show the spectators the organized game of soccer, beginning to end?

Think about your favorite movies and/or classic stories. Common plots and/or themes that have been identified include the "Cinderella" type—a person perceived to be of no value but actually being of great value, a fugitive, a quest, coming of age, love conquers, thwarted love, etc. Ask yourself the following questions:

- What types of characters are in the story? Are any characters always perfect or completely evil? What types of characters recur?
- What are the patterns in the story?
- What does the main character want? What problems or challenges does he or she encounter? What are the steps in the process as the hero or heroine tries to solve the problem and meet the challenge?
- Who helps or hinders the main character along the way?
- Is there any danger?
- What role does the antagonist play?
- How does the character overcome the difficulty?
- How does the story end? Does it always end "happily ever after?" Does the hero or heroine reach the desired goal? Why or why not? Is there more than one part to the conclusion?

Identify these elements and the scenes that take place in the story you chose to consider. Plot them on the story map on the next page. Try this again on a separate piece of paper, using your own characters, settings, problem or challenge, etc., but using the same plot style you just mapped out. Write out your story, using the plot line prompts as a guide.

Check Yourself

What common patterns did you find in the movie or classic story model? How did organizing the pieces of the story first help you in your writing?

> **My Notes**
> _____   _____
> _____   _____
> _____   _____
> _____   _____

Classic Strategy

1. The main character or hero is in his or her own ordinary world.	2. The hero is asked to leave his or her comfort zone; this day will not be ordinary. The hero is presented with a problem or challenge, something he or she has to solve, perhaps something he or she must obtain.	3. The hero doesn't want to do the task. There may also be a fear of the unknown.
4. Someone comes along and gives the hero advice, encouragement, or tools the hero will need. The hero must still solve the problem on his or her own. The help may come from a person, or it may come from something the hero reads.	5. The adventure begins for the hero. He or she is required to be in a new setting and may not be sure how to get there.	6. The main character faces various problems. How will the hero react under stress? What tests and other obstacles will he or she face?
7. Obstacles grow more difficult; the hero finds himself or herself in trouble, in a dangerous place (physical or otherwise).	8. The hero tries many things, none of which seems to work. He or she faces the end of his or her options and struggles for survival.	9. The hero solves the problem; he or she now has met the challenge, obtained the prize.
10. As the main character faced obstacles, there may have been consequences. The hero must now deal with these consequences.	11. The main character faces one last obstacle or ordeal. Your hero must survive this one as well. This need not be a happy ending, but it must make sense and be satisfactory.	12. The hero returns to his or her ordinary world with the problem solved. He or she may also bring back whatever he or she obtained on the journey (new knowledge, prize, understanding, etc.).

Conventions Trait

A word formerly used for *conventions* is *mechanics*; teachers at one time referred to the "mechanics of writing." Some baseball players refer to the "mechanics" of playing the game. This section explores baseball players, the equipment they use, the methods they use to improve their game, and how those methods relate to writing. Conventions are a writer's tools to keep a story flowing smoothly. Editing is a huge task; students will learn the process by using one tool at a time. They will find that it takes practice to become familiar with using the tools.

Baseball players and coaches review games on video, analyzing plays for consistency. Batters constantly review and edit their game to maintain control of the bat. Pitchers review and practice to keep their arm motions consistent. Runners calculate exactly how far off base they can lead with the least likelihood they will be picked off. When each player reviews, edits, and works to improve his or her play, it results in a winning team.

Conventions, as identified in this trait model, include spelling, punctuation, capitalization, grammar, paragraphs, and using appropriate titles. The teacher may also address repetition or overuse of words, the correct use of "that" and "which," using active verbs instead of "to be" verbs, and using descriptive nouns to cut down on overuse of adjectives.

In the first lesson, students will be introduced to the conventions and practice editing writing samples, using the common proofreading marks shown on page 58. You may wish to copy the first writing sample onto an overhead transparency and use it to review the common proofreading marks with your class before they begin editing. After students edit the sample paragraphs, they will write their own paragraphs. Collect these paragraphs, remove student names, and/or any other identification (you may wish to type the samples if students know their classmates' handwriting) for use in the third exercise. In the remaining exercises, students will continue to practice editing others' work, individually and in a group activity. Students will then begin to practice editing passages they have written while studying the previous traits. Finally, students will thoroughly edit a piece of their writing for "publication," or presentation, using a levels-of-revision checklist shown on page 67.

Conventions

(to the student)

You've reached the home stretch—last inning, runners on base, set for the home run that will win the game. Baseball players and coaches review games on video, analyzing plays for consistency. Batters constantly review and edit their game to maintain control of the bat. Pitchers review and practice to keep their arm motions consistent. Runners calculate exactly how far off base they can lead with the least likelihood they will be picked off. Each player reviewing, editing, and working to improve his or her play will result in a winning team.

Conventions are the equipment and mechanics of writing. This is the part of the process when you will focus on correcting errors, improving your writing, and polishing it to a smooth, finished work. This process does not happen all at once; it occurs over time, as you give it all you have and push yourself to reach your potential. Through daily routines, you will develop consistent editing skills. Success at baseball—and writing—requires confidence, trust, an inner belief in yourself and your abilities.

Baseball is a sport that requires specific equipment. Conventions, as one of the traits of good writing, include spelling, punctuation, capitalization, grammar, paragraphs, and using appropriate titles, as well as overall revision of your writing.

Check Your Conventions

- Use correct spelling.
- Use correct capitalization.
- Use correct punctuation.
- Use proper grammar.
- Use effective paragraphs.
- Use appropriate titles.
- Avoid needless repetition, overuse of words.
- Maintain correct word usage—e.g., "that" and "which."
- Use active verbs instead of "to be" verbs.
- Use descriptive nouns rather than adjectives.
- Make sure it passes the read aloud test.
- Make every word and sentence necessary with nothing extra.

Proofreading Marks

Throughout this text, the process of proofreading is suggested as a vital step in the writing process. To be sure that all students use the same "language" when editing their papers and their peers' papers, the following list of marks has been provided:

Editor's Mark	Meaning	Example
ℓ	Delete	It was ~~was~~ very tiny.
≡	Capitalize	<u>the</u> boy ran quickly.
/	Use lowercase	Many /Athletes ran in the marathon.
∧	Add a word	I want an ice ∧ sundae. (cream)
RO	Run-on sentence	Who's there^RO what do you want?
frag.	Sentence fragment	Although the peddler's cart. frag.
SP	Spelling error	Monkies^SP swung in the trees.
∽	Reverse letters or words	Five books on were the shlef.
⊙	Add a period	Children played all day⊙
∧ (comma)	Add a comma	I like apples∧peaches, and pears.
∨	Add an apostrophe	John∨s puppy is cute.
∨ (open) ∨ (close)	Add quotation marks	∨Help!∨ I cried.
¶	Begin a new paragraph	"Hello," said Carla.¶ "Hi," Beth replied.
#	Make a space	I love French#fries.
⌣	Close the space	He lives in the country ⌣ side.
stet	Do not delete (Let it stand.)	The ~~beautiful~~ swan flew away. (stet)

Warming Up

Equipment

- copy of Proofreading Marks, page 58
- writing notebook and materials

Trait Development

Editing is something you will do over and over again as you learn to revise and improve your writing. Baseball players practice batting, catching, and pitching repeatedly to improve their game. When you edit your writing, it helps to make notes to yourself so you will remember what you need to correct when writing the final copy. Many editors use common proofreading marks as reminders; these are listed on page 58. Practice using those proofreading marks as you edit the writing samples below. Edit for the conventions of spelling, capitalization, punctuation, grammar, and paragraphs. Give the paragraphs an appropriate title.

Write your own paragraph about baseball. Give your paragraph to your teacher.

Check Yourself

How does writing that needs editing compare to a baseball player's development of his or her skills? When editing a piece of writing, what is meant by conventions? Which aspects of your own writing do you find most difficult to edit? Which are the easiest? Why?

Sample #1 (*nine corrections*) _____
(*Title*)

Enyone can play baseball. it does not matter how big or tall you are, as long as you gives your best effort. Believe in yourself and set goals. The diffirence between a good baseball player and a poor one is focus. Concentrate on Playing the game well. Continue to praktice and learn, and you will meet you're goal of be a sucessful player.

Sample #2 (*nine corrections*) _____
(*Title*)

Baseball are a great sport. The equipment is expensive, but its worth it. People play baseball, to have fun and exircise. A baseball is usally white with stitching of another color. Baseball players wear safety equipment so they will not get hurt. for example, the batter wears a helmet and the catcher wears a catchers' mask. The Pitcher throws the ball to the batter, who tries to hit the ball and runs around as many bases as he can. Every person at bat hopes for a home run. Many people think baseball is the best American sport.

The Pitch

Tip from the Coach

Focus on one aspect of editing at a time.

Equipment

- colored pencils
- writing sample, pages 61, 62, and 63

Trait Development

The baseball batter needs to focus on one pitch at a time. Each pitch gives the batter the opportunity to get a hit, strike, or a ball. The batter must analyze each pitch to determine the speed, whether it's an inside or an outside pitch, a straight or curve ball. Similarly, you will also consider several things when editing a piece of writing. You will focus on one aspect at a time as you edit the writing sample on pages 61–63. Begin with spelling. Select a colored pencil and go through the first section of the sample, correcting only for spelling. Circle any misspelled words and write the correct spelling above the misspelled word. Use a different colored pencil to edit the next section of the piece again, focusing on the next convention—capitalization. When you edit for grammar, remember to check for words that are spelled correctly but used incorrectly in a sentence. Go through this process for each aspect to be edited. Give the story an appropriate title.

Check Yourself

Rewrite the story. How did the editing changes you made improve the writing? How did it feel to edit this way, focusing on one convention at a time? Why is it easier to tackle the process of editing one step at a time?

My Notes

_____   _____

_____   _____

_____   _____

_____   _____

_____   _____

_____   _____

_____   _____

_____   _____

_____   _____

_____   _____

The Pitch *(cont.)*

Writing Sample

Directions: Edit the following writing sample (*pages 61–63*).

Spelling: *Find eight spelling errors. Write the word correctly above the incorrectly spelled word.*

Mike tugged on his batting glove and dug in for the pich. This was the momint he had longed for. The score was tied, with two runners in the scoring posiion at the bottom of the final ining.

Two years ago Mike had been in his first year of Babe Ruth legue and he had struck out in a big game. He never forgot it. He knew it was "just a game," but he felt he had let everybody down. His teamates hadn't seemed to care. Mom and Dad had allways been supportive. But Mike had cared—mabe too much, he thought.

Capitalization: *Find eight capitalization errors. Use the proofreading marks to make corrections.*

Mike loved this time of year. but baseball made it even more special. Summer meant throwing and catching, pitching and batting, and running bases. It meant Pick-up Games with his Friends until it was too dark to see the ball. even a lot of girls played in those games; some of them were really good and played hard.

Mike had faced this pitcher Before. A tall, left-handed pitcher, he threw hard, and mike always thought it looked like the ball would hit him. earlier in the game he had hit Mike with a pitch, and now Mike wanted a hit of his own.

The Pitch *(cont.)*

Writing Sample *(cont.)*

Punctuation: *Find six punctuation errors. Use the proofreading marks to make corrections.*

The tall lefty wound up and let the first pitch fly. It buzzed by low and outside. Ball one

For as long as he could remember there had always been pictures and home videos of him as a

toddler, swinging a plastic bat and throwing his whiffle ball. Born to play ball" Mike always

thought about himself. He had played T-ball, and Little League before Babe Ruth league.

Grammar: *Find seven grammar errors. Circle the error and write the words correctly above the incorrect words.*

Another pitch speed towards home plate and Mike swung—he fouled it over the backstop.

The count evened at "one and one."

Baseball had it's own set of problems. Torn and grass-stained blue jeans often drew scowls

for his mother. Mike had missing lunches and been late for dinner more than once. Once too

often, his dad had to pay for a broken window from a long fly ball off Mike's bat has led to

extra yard work. None of this bothered Mike. It was baseball.

What was this? A change-up or a curve ball? It was a lot slower pitch. Mike's eyes widened

and he started to swing. But he stopped and let the ball go by, too low. That was a pitch he

wanted crush. A little smile cross his face. "I'd like that pitch again," he thought.

The Pitch *(cont.)*

Writing Sample *(cont.)*

Paragraphs: *Find three paragraph breaks and show them, using proofreader's marks.*

Yeah, Mike thinks about it. Playing in the big leagues. He and his father go to minor league games, and he can easily see himself on the field. He sees himself playing in the World Series, playing in front of thousands of fans. He always makes the diving catch and gets the big hit. The pitcher's best fastball headed toward Mike. He swung and hit a ground ball—just past the outstretched glove of the diving shortstop. A base hit! The runners advanced and Mike made it to first base, but no runners scored. Not quite a hero, Mike played hard and helped his team. He got his hit and had fun while his team won a big game. He didn't remember what was for dinner after the game. But he does recall running out the door, with the last bite in his mouth, carrying his bat and glove into the evening for another big game of baseball.

—Robert Petty (*used with author's permission*)

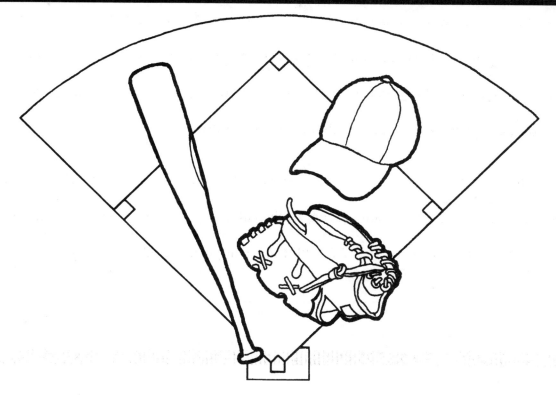

You Swing . . .

Tip from the Coach

Continue to practice, and you will become familiar with the editing process.

Equipment

- colored pencil
- sample paragraph

Trait Development

Your teacher will give you a sample paragraph written by one of your classmates. Edit the sample paragraph you have received. Focus on one convention at a time, as you did in the previous exercise. Use a different-colored pencil for each convention. Remember to use the common proofreading marks as well. If the piece needs a title, create an appropriate title. Return the paper to its original author. When you receive your edited paragraph, rewrite it as a final copy, making the corrections noted.

Check Yourself

How did it feel to edit the work of someone you know? How is the editing process becoming easier? Did you agree or disagree with your classmate's suggestions for editing your paragraph? Why or why not? How has your writing improved?

My Notes

One Base at a Time

Tip from the Coach

Practice editing basics to improve your writing.

Equipment

- colored pencils
- a piece of your writing from a previous exercise or assignment

Trait Development

Choose a piece of your writing that you really would like to revise. Before you begin editing, read the "Essentials of Editing" listed below. Use the same process you used in the previous exercise: select a colored pencil and go through the entire sample, correcting only for spelling. Use a different colored pencil to edit the piece again, focusing on another convention—e.g., grammar. Go through this process for each aspect to be edited. Also mark those places in your writing where your reader might stumble, using a colored pencil to catch your attention.

Check Yourself

Rewrite your story. How did the editing changes improve your writing? How did it feel to edit your work? How did reviewing the "Essentials of Editing" help your perspective as you worked?

Essentials of Editing

- Take responsibility for your writing.
- Commit to your purpose: know how you want your writing to look and what you want to accomplish.
- Make your editing consistent with your goals.
- Edit one line at a time.
- Remain confident, believe in your ability.
- Stay focused on the process of editing.
- Remember you can't control critical comments, but you can control your response, and you can control how you improve your writing.
- Develop your editing skills so you can write to the best of your ability.
- Practice.
- Learn something new.
- Keep it simple.

My Notes

_____   _____

_____   _____

_____   _____

_____

Home Run

Equipment

- a piece of your writing you would like to edit, either the piece used in the previous exercise or another piece
- Levels of Revision, page 67

Trait Development

You've learned to use many pieces of equipment, or tools, in editing. Practicing consistently will help you develop your skills. Just as baseball players review a game over and over again, each time focusing on a different aspect of their play, analyzing your work at different levels will improve your writing.

Writing can be revised at more than one level as well. One author stated the process simply: "Read it, change it. Read it, change it. Read it, change it." Let's look at some specifics.

Make sure your writing is in a format with plenty of white space to make changes. Begin with Level #1 on the next page, Levels of Revision. Look over your story, keeping only those suggestions in mind. Next, read Level #2, and read through your story again, making changes only at this level. Continue through each level, revising your work as you go.

Check Yourself

Rewrite your story, incorporating the revisions you made.

My Notes

_____   _____

_____   _____

_____   _____

_____   _____

_____   _____

_____   _____

_____   _____

_____   _____

_____   _____

Levels of Revision

Level #1

- Let the piece sit overnight—or longer if possible.
- Read the piece all the way through.
- Read it. Change it. Read it. Change it.
- Does it sound complete? Are there any parts missing?

Level #2

- Look a little closer.
- Check the focus.
- Cut out whatever does not relate to the main topic.
- Does the ending answer any questions raised in the beginning?
- Does the piece say what you intended it to say?

Level #3

- Is the piece logically organized?
- Cut out any self-conscious writing.
- Remember that your reader will filter your writing through his or her personal experience.
- Read it aloud. Cut out anything that doesn't sound right.

Level #4

- Look at the details.
- Read it aloud, slowly.
- Look for awkward sentence structure.
- Check for any long sentences that should be two sentences instead.
- Does every line add to the whole?

Level #5

- Cut out any extra words that don't add to the whole.
- Change and/or add words for clarification.
- Look for repeated words. Use a thesaurus to add interest.
- Look up words to check meanings and spellings.
- "Line edit"—make sure every sentence, phrase, or word says what you want it to say.

Presentation Trait

A writer's purpose is to convey a message. The way that message is communicated will determine how well the audience receives it. A story may be well-written but still be ineffective if it lacks qualities of the presentation trait.

Track and field is a sport focused on presentation. A track and field athlete knows that the start can affect the outcome of an event. The athlete must run with confidence, learn to make up for mistakes, plan to win, and continue on through the finish. In like manner, the writer presents his or her work using auditory and/or visual methods. When presenting orally, the writer maintains eye contact, speaks clearly, and uses a normal rate and volume. Ideas must be organized to convey main points to the audience. The writer must start strong, have confidence, plan to do well, and continue to the end, even if mistakes are made.

Track and field athletes develop styles of running, jumping, and throwing. The goal is accuracy and excellence. Visually, students' presentation of writing is similar to an athlete's performance. A presentation will use illustrations to catch one's attention and visual aids related to the topic, expressing ideas and reflections with accuracy and excellence.

In these lessons, students use various activities to present their work to others. In the first exercise, students create a visual presentation of names. If you use computers, you may wish to have students use the "Scrolling Marquee" option in Windows to create a screen-saver design using their names (My Computer/Control Panel/Display/Screen Saver).

Next, students observe weather and present observations. You may wish to incorporate small-group presentations, using dance, rhythmic movements, drama, as well as verbal, written, and other artistic methods. Students write and give a speech in the next lesson. In the next exercise, students create presentations using scrapbook techniques to add to a short piece of their writing. Have magazine advertisements and a variety of craft supplies on hand, as well as sample scrapbook pages. You may wish to discuss elements of graphic design in the ads. In the final lesson, students will "publish" their writing for others. You may want to show samples of student-published work—stories bound with staples or bindings, presentation boards, booklets, brochures, etc. Also, allow students to create a multi-media presentation for this exercise. Options might include PowerPoint, video cameras, digital cameras, and/or desktop publishing programs. A culminating activity incorporates all of the traits. Students work in groups to "sponsor" an event, as if for a track meet. This activity may also be presented to family members at an Open House.

Presentation

(to the student)

This is the big event, and you want to be prepared. You will be presenting your writing to others, and you want to impress them. Your goals will be the same as those of the track and field athlete—accuracy, excellence, and accomplishment.

Track and field is a sport that develops a variety of skills—running, throwing, jumping. To do your best, you need to know yourself and your abilities, to become familiar with the course and pace yourself. As a writer, you will set similar goals. When presenting your work, you need to think about what styles work best for you. You will consider whether you are an auditory person or whether you rely more on visual cues. You will want to know what your audience requires of you.

Become familiar with the characteristics of the presentation trait. Writing that is presented effectively will include illustrations that catch the eye, such as photos, drawings, charts, maps, or graphs. Present such visual aids attractively, using colors, various text styles, and layout designs. Express your own ideas and reflections just as track and field athletes develop their own styles of running, jumping, and throwing.

A track and field athlete knows that how one starts can affect the outcome of a race. One must run with confidence, learn to make up for mistakes, plan to win, and continue on through the finish. When you present work orally, you need to start strongly, have confidence, plan to do well, and continue to the end, even if you make mistakes. Learn to maintain eye contact, speak clearly, and use a normal rate and volume. Organize your thoughts and ideas to convey your main points to your audience.

Remember These Elements of Presentation

Visual Elements

- Select a presentation format.
- Include illustrations that catch the reader's attention.
- Incorporate visual aids, such as photos, drawings, charts, and graphs.
- Express your own ideas and reflections.

Auditory Elements

- Tell about personal experiences and/or knowledge of the topic.
- Ask and respond to questions.
- Have a clear main point when speaking to others.
- Read your writing to others.
- Make eye contact while giving oral presentations.
- Organize your ideas for oral presentations (include content appropriate to the audience, use notes or other memory aids, summarize main points).

Introducing . . .

Tip from the Coach

In a track meet, each athlete is introduced.

Equipment

- colored pencils or markers
- construction paper

Trait Development

What does it mean to present yourself? to perform? What does it mean to present your writing? Athletes in track and field perform visually before spectators. They present their personal best. Brainstorm ways that authors present their writing. Stop now and list your ideas.

Authors might write books, screenplays for movies, give speeches, tell stories, and create graphic art on clothing and other items.

You will create a small poster to "present" your name. Practice the characteristics of the presentation trait, focusing on expressing your own ideas and reflections. You may wish to use glitter, markers, or other visual media if available. You may also wish to create a screen saver design featuring your name using the "Scrolling Marquee" option available in Windows.

If you have time, write a paragraph about yourself, titled "I Am . . . ," or "Presenting . . . (your name)." Don't sign your name; when the paragraphs are displayed around the room, see if you can tell which of your classmates wrote each piece.

Check Yourself

Were you able to tell your classmates' writing by their personalities? How did you feel about your presentation of your name? How did this activity help you begin to familiarize yourself with qualities of the presentation trait?

My Notes

_____   _____

_____   _____

_____   _____

_____   _____

_____   _____

_____   _____

_____   _____

_____   _____

Presenting . . .

Equipment

- clipboard
- colored pencils

Trait Development

(*Your teacher may have you work in small groups for part of this activity.*)

Track and field focuses on competition and presentation of the athlete's abilities. As an author, you will present your writing so that others can see and hear your talent, abilities, and ideas. Before a meet, the athlete trains and prepares for a variety of possible circumstances, including weather.

You will observe weather, nature's presentation, and then design your own presentation to share with others. If the weather permits, take a clipboard outside and observe the weather and other elements of the outdoors. How does nature present itself? If the weather is too inclement, observe through the window.

Refer to your observations to prepare your presentation. If possible, work with a small group and create a dramatic presentation, using movement and/or music.

Check Yourself

What did you learn about the presentation trait by observing nature? How did working with a group help you become familiar with aspects of this trait?

My Notes

_____   _____
_____   _____
_____   _____
_____   _____
_____   _____
_____   _____
_____   _____
_____   _____

The Athletes Speak

Equipment

- index cards
- Visual Aid Samples (page 73)

Trait Development

When working with a team, a coach will often give the athletes tips and advice. He or she may demonstrate concepts visually, using visual aids such as diagrams or charts. The coach is speaking to a group of people, in this case, the team. As a writer, you may also be called upon to speak to a group of people—to share your work, thoughts, and ideas with others.

Usually, those who speak publicly to a group of people write the speech before they present it. When writing a speech, you will need to choose a topic, have at least three main points, or things you wish to say about your topic, and include a visual aid. A visual aid is something that gives information about your topic or helps you explain it. You will also need to introduce your topic and write a conclusion to your speech.

Brainstorm possible topics for your speech. You may wish to use a web or cluster graphic organizer to get ideas. Possible topics might include sports, animals, school, activities, hobbies, or topics of special interest.

On the first index card, write your topic. Use three additional index cards to write the main points in your speech. You may also want to write one or two specific details and/or examples about each point to remind yourself of what you want to say. Decide which type of visual aid will be most appropriate for your topic and make some notes on a fifth index card.

Design your visual aid, using markers, construction paper, computer-generated graphics, presentation boards, magazine pictures or other photos, or other visual media appropriate for your speech. Practice your speech before you present it to the class.

Check Yourself

What qualities made the speeches you heard given by your classmates effective? What was the easiest part of preparing a speech? the most difficult? How do visual aids help the listener understand the speaker's main points?

My Notes

_____   _____

_____   _____

_____   _____

_____   _____

_____   _____

Visual Aid Samples

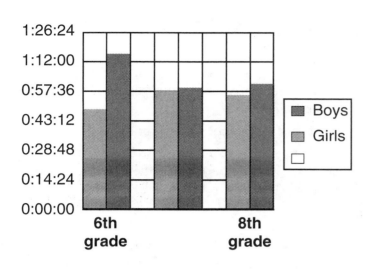

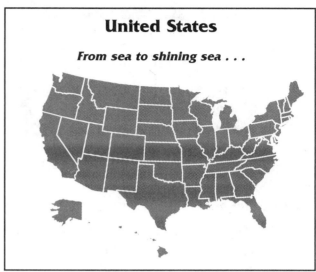

United States

From sea to shining sea . . .

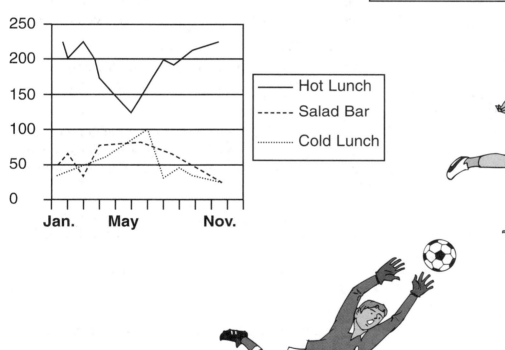

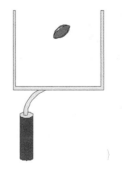

Track and Field— a Collage of Events

Tip from the Coach

A variety of materials may be used to create a presentation.

Equipment

- a short piece of your writing you wish to present visually to others
- craft scissors, rulers with decorative edges
- shape templates, colored construction paper, stickers (if available), magazine advertisements (optional)

Trait Development

Track and field incorporates a variety of visual elements, such as running, jumping, throwing, etc. A track meet often has many events occurring at the same time. The spectator watches this collage, focusing on one event, then another.

Examine magazine advertisements, observing the page layout and design. Notice the use of color, letter styles, and placement of text and illustrations on the page. If sample scrapbook pages are available, study those as well, observing the use of color, shape, and design layout.

Select a short piece of your writing that you would like to illustrate visually and present to others. If you don't have a writing sample, write two or three paragraphs about your favorite sport. Make sure your chosen piece is a final copy, already edited and copied neatly or typed. Create a "scrapbook" page using your writing, incorporating the principles of page layout and design you have observed. Present your work to the class.

Check Yourself

What made various presentations interesting? How did effective presentations incorporate qualities of the presentation trait?

My Notes

_____   _____

_____   _____

_____   _____

_____   _____

_____   _____

_____   _____

_____   _____

Your Presentation . . .

Tip from the Coach

Run a good race—all the way to the finish.

Equipment

- a rough draft of a piece of your writing
- presentation boards, construction paper, markers, colored pencils, glue, tagboard, and/or similar art supplies as needed

Trait Development

Brainstorm different ways that writing may be presented. What types of presentation have you seen in the previous lessons? Discuss as a class what elements make presentation of writing effective. Remember such features as color, title, word style, illustrations, graphics, layout of page, types of bindings, etc. Decide how you would like to present your writing.

Begin with your rough draft. Edit and revise your work, making any necessary changes. Write or type a final copy. Design and create the final published format for your written work. You may choose to publish your work as a bound story, booklet, or folder story. Or, you may choose to make a presentation board or brochures to go with your writing.

Present your work to the class and/or others in the community. You may want to give your story to a younger class or as a gift to a family member. You could donate a nonfiction presentation board or brochure to your school or classroom library as a resource. What other ways can you share your work with others?

Check Yourself

How did it feel to complete a piece of writing, from start to finish? What do you like about your published work/presentation? What would you do differently next time? What makes the editing and publishing process worth the effort?

My Notes

_____   _____

_____   _____

_____   _____

_____   _____

_____   _____

_____   _____

_____   _____

All-Star Track Meet

Equipment

- samples of your writing and other presentations
- presentation and display materials and supplies

Trait Development

By now, you have learned much about effective writing and how to present your work to others. It's time to display your work to those outside your class.

Work cooperatively in groups to create a visual, auditory, or dramatic presentation. Remember to incorporate various aspects of the presentation trait. You will need to include at least a title, visual images, and written text in your display, and possibly an auditory presentation as well. You may use multi-media devices such as PowerPoint, digital cameras, video cameras or other recording devices, and/or desktop publishing programs as they are available to you.

Plan the overall presentation. What "event" (or part of the Open House program) will each group be responsible for? How will you set up the displays? Plan any necessary decorations. Decide whom you will invite and how you will get the necessary information to your guests.

As you prepare your display, consider what you will say to your spectators. How will you present your work orally?

If time allows, give your classmates positive feedback about the traits of effective writing that you noticed in their presentations and displays.

Check Yourself

Review the traits of effective writing you have studied and practiced. Which trait will be easiest for you to continue to incorporate into your writing? Why? Which is the most difficult? What have you learned that will help you develop these characteristics in your writing?

My Notes

_____   _____

_____   _____

_____   _____

_____   _____

_____   _____

_____   _____

Answer Key

What's the Strategy?, page 49.

1. The oldest known team sport in the world is soccer.

2. In the game of soccer, team members work together to control the ball and set up scoring opportunities.

3. Each team member must be aware of where other players are on the field.

4. It is also important for each person to play his or her position.

5. Soccer is a game of running, quick speed, clear thinking, and focusing on the goal.

6. People around the world enjoy this fast paced game of action.

Warming Up, page 59

Sample #1 (eight corrections)

Anyone can play baseball. **It** does not matter how big or tall you are, as long as you **give** your best effort. Believe in yourself and set goals. The **difference** between a good baseball player and a poor one is focus. Concentrate on **playing** the game well. Continue to **practice** and learn, and you will meet **your** goal of **being** a **successful** player.

Sample #2 (nine corrections)

Baseball **is** a great sport. The equipment is expensive, but **it's** worth it. People play baseball (*Omit comma.*) to have fun and **exercise**. A baseball is **usually** white with stitching of another color. Baseball players wear safety equipment so they will not get hurt. **For** example, the batter wears a helmet and the catcher wears a **catcher's** mask. The **pitcher** throws the ball to the batter, who tries to hit the ball and **run** around as many bases as he can. Every person at bat hopes for a home run. Many people think baseball is the best American sport.

The Pitch, pages 61–63

Writing Sample

Spelling: *Find eight spelling errors. Write the word correctly above the incorrectly spelled word.*

Mike tugged on his batting glove and dug in for the **pitch**. This was the **moment** he had longed for. The score was tied, with two runners in the scoring **position**, at the bottom of the final **inning**.

Two years ago Mike had been in his first year of Babe Ruth **league** and he had struck out in a big game. He never forgot it. He knew it was "just a game," but he felt he had let everybody down. His **teammates** hadn't seemed to care. Mom and Dad had **always** been supportive. But Mike had cared— **maybe** too much, he thought.

Answer Key *(cont.)*

Capitalization: *Find eight errors. Use the proofreading marks to make corrections.*

Mike loved this time of year. **But** baseball made it even more special. Summer meant throwing and catching, pitching and batting, and running bases. It meant **pick-up games** with his **friends** until it was too dark to see the ball. **Even** a lot of girls played in those games; some of them were really good and played hard.

Mike had faced this pitcher **before**. A tall, left-handed pitcher, he threw hard, and **Mike** always thought it looked as if the ball would hit him. **Earlier** in the game he had hit Mike with a pitch, and now Mike wanted a hit of his own.

Punctuation: *Find six punctuation errors. Use the proofreading marks to make corrections.*

The tall lefty wound up and let the first pitch fly. It buzzed by low and outside. Ball one. *(Add period.)*

For as long as he could remember, *(Add comma.)* there had always been pictures and home videos of him as a toddler *(Omit comma.)* swinging a plastic bat and throwing his whiffle ball. *(Add quote mark.)* "Born to play ball," *(Add comma.)* Mike always thought about himself. He had played T-ball and Little League before Babe Ruth League. *(Capitalize L.)*

Grammar: *Find seven grammar errors. Circle the error and write the word(s) correctly above the incorrect word(s).*

Another pitch **sped** towards home plate and Mike swung—he fouled it over the backstop. The count evened at "one and one."

Baseball had **its** own set of problems. Torn and grass-stained blue jeans often drew scowls **from** his mother. Mike had **missed** lunches and been late for dinner more than once. Once too often, his dad had to pay for a broken window from a long fly ball off Mike's bat **had** led to extra yard work. None of this bothered Mike. It was baseball.

What was this? A change-up or a curve ball? It was a lot slower pitch. Mike's eyes widened and he started to swing. But he stopped and let the ball go by, too low. That was a pitch he wanted **to** crush. A little smile **crossed** his face. "I'd like that pitch again," he thought.

Paragraphs: *Find three paragraph breaks and show them, using proofreader's marks.*

P   Yeah, Mike thinks about it. Playing in the big leagues. He and his father go to minor league games, and he can easily see himself on the field. He sees himself playing in the World Series, playing in front of thousands of fans. He always makes the diving catch and gets the big hit.

P   The pitcher's best fastball headed toward Mike. He swung and hit a ground ball—just past the outstretched glove of the diving shortstop. A base hit! The runners advanced and Mike made it to first base, but no runners scored.

P   Not quite a hero, Mike played hard and helped his team. He got his hit and had fun while his team won a big game. He didn't remember what was for dinner after the game. But he does recall running out the door, with the last bite in his mouth, carrying his bat and glove into the evening for another big game of baseball.

—Robert Petty *(used with author's permission)*

Technology Resources

Microsoft Publisher 97 (or later version). Microsoft Corporation.

(desktop publishing program)

The program enables students to incorporate original text with clip art to create their own publications.

Microsoft Word 97 (or later version). Microsoft Corporation.

(word processing program)

Word also allows students to add clip art to their documents. It is easy to enter text and edit. The "insert comment" and "auto correct" features allow teachers to disable automatic corrections of common student errors and to edit and comment on student work.

Microsoft PowerPoint. Microsoft Corporation.

(desktop publishing and multi-media presentation program)

Students create presentations that may be printed out for teacher review and/or presented to the class as a slide show using a computer projector system. Slides may include clip art, digital or scanned photographs, charts, and graphs as well as text.

Claris Works

(integrated task program)

An all-in-one application that includes word processing, spreadsheet, database, painting, and graphics modules. It also includes an extensive clip art library and several templates to help with common writing tasks. This program is available for both PCs and MacIntosh computers, but is most often used with MacIntosh computers.

Kid Pix. The Learning Company

(a paint, draw, and graphics program)

Internet Web Sites

Merriam-Webster Online

http://www.m-w.com

This site features an online dictionary and thesaurus.

edHelper.com

http://www.edhelper.com

This site has word puzzles and work sheets covering a variety of themes.

Teachers.Net

http://www.teachers.net

A valuable resource for teachers, this site includes many language arts lesson plans.

National Council of Teachers of English Homepage

http://www.ncte.org

This site offers a variety of language arts resources for teachers, including book lists and lesson plans.

Bibliography

Arnold, Caroline. *Soccer: From Neighborhood Play to the World Cup*. Franklin Watts, 1991.

Boyle, Doe. *Otter on His Own*: *The Story of a Sea Otter*. Soundprints, 1995.

Carlstrom, Nancy W. *Swim the Silver Sea, Joshie Otter*. Philomel Books, 1993.

Christopher, Matt. *Olympic Dream*. Little, Brown, & Co., 1996.

Elling, R. M. *The All-Mountain Skier*: *The Way to Expert Skiing*. McGraw-Hill Trade, 2002.

George, Jean Craighead. *Cliff Hanger*. HarperCollins, 2002.

George, Jean Craighead. *Shark Beneath the Reef*. HarperTrophy, 1989.

Heskett, Tracie. *Using the Six-Trait Writing Model*. Teacher Created Materials, 2001.

Heskett, Tracie. *Using the Traits of Good Writing*. Teacher Created Materials, 2003.

Italia, Bob. *Snowboarding*. ABDO Publishing Co. 1991.

Jackson, Colin. *The Young Track and Field Athlete*. DK Publishing, 1996.

Klinzing, James and Michael Klinzing. *Fundamental Basketball*. Lerner Publications Co., 1996.

Knox, Barbara. *BMX Bikes*. Capstone Press, 1996.

McKenna, Lesley. *The Fantastic Book of Snowboarding*. Millbrook Press, 1998.

Ominsky, D. and P. J. Harari. *Soccer Made Simple: A Spectator's Guide*. First Base Sports, 1994.

Ravizza, K. and T. Hanson. *Heads-Up Baseball: Playing the Game One Pitch at a Time*. McGraw-Hill, 1998.

Rosenthal, Bert. *Track and Field*. Raintree Steck-Vaughn, 1994.

Stewart, Peter. *Way to Play Soccer*. Prima Publishing, 1995.

Stone, Tanya L. and Samuel G. Woods. *Snowboards: From Start to Finish*. Gale, 2000.

Thomas, David G. *Swimming: Steps to Success*. Human Kinetics Publishers, 1996.

Wooldridge, Susan G. *poemcrazy*: *Freeing Your Life with Words*. Random House Value. 1997.